JOURNAL KEEPING
with
YOUNG PEOPLE

JOURNAL KEEPING
with
YOUNG PEOPLE

Barbara Steiner
and
Kathleen C. Phillips
Illustrated by Robert B. Phillips

1991

TEACHER IDEAS PRESS
A Division of
Libraries Unlimited, Inc.
Englewood, Colorado

TEACHER IDEAS PRESS
A Division of
Libraries Unlimited, Inc.
P.O. Box 3988
Englewood, CO 80155-3988

Library of Congress Cataloging-in-Publication Data

Steiner, Barbara A.
    Journal keeping with young people / Barbara Steiner and Kathleen
C. Phillips : illustrated by Robert B. Phillips.
    xiii, 185 p. 17x25 cm.
    Includes bibliographical references and index.
    ISBN 0-87287-872-4
    1. Language arts (Elementary) 2. Diaries--Authorship. 3. English
language--Composition and exercises--Study and teaching.
I. Phillips, Kathleen C. II. Title.
LB1576.S788 1991
372.6--dc20
                                                    91-8766
                                                      CIP

To Phyllis A. Whitney

*Who, whether she has known it or not,
has been mentor for both of us since
the beginning of our writing careers*

Contents

Preface

In schools we have visited, we have noticed that teachers are using journal keeping with children more and more. We have inquired whether teachers would like a book that expanded their ideas on journal keeping, that gave them more specific techniques on journaling. Would they like suggestions for using material gained from journals, while making sure children have the privacy they need to write freely? The answer was an emphatic yes.

Journal keeping is so much more than just a logging in of daily events. A journal can appreciate and enjoy the present, but it can also recall the past, explore the future, enrich relationships, help solve problems. It can provide a catharsis for strong emotion, or be a place for reflection and introspection. It can be used to build a rich fantasy life. We can take a look at the people closest to us and also study and enjoy people in general. A journal can help us learn to live with those people and share our home, Planet Earth, in positive ways. We can write fiction in a journal, but fiction so closely based on our real lives that we do not care to share it at this time. The journal is certainly a place to celebrate life in all the diverse ways it comes to us.

Psychologists think that childhood memories reveal adult personalities, especially memories that haven't been taken out and dealt with. Hitler remembers his father beating him. He kept all the anger from these beatings inside until he took it out on nations of people. We make no claim that if he had written about this anger, tried to understand it, tried to understand why his father beat him, that he would have totally rid himself of his anger. We can't say he wouldn't have been goaded by that anger to abuse the power he later acquired. But we do know that childhood memories can be channeled into fiction, that one can rid oneself of negative memories. We have seen many students deal with hidden anger, hostility, and past hurt through writing out these emotions in a journal.

Many times students come to us and say, "You have changed my life." (For the better, we hope, and this is usually the case.) We cannot take credit for doing this. The student has changed his or her own life by writing about it to make it better, by discovering patterns from the past that need to be changed today. They have learned to focus on joy instead of pain. They have solved some life problems so that they could move forward. They have been able to make transitions into a new phase of living. And they have done this not by magic, but by writing day after day in their journals, by letting us guide them on paths they were afraid to follow or that they didn't know were there.

In this book we will endeavor to explore all these journal possibilities and offer exercises that will motivate young people to write about themselves in a deep and personal way. The exercises are aimed at upper elementary and middle school students but could be adapted for younger children or high school students. We have tried to keep in mind the activities and interests of these ages, but have also used exercises to stretch the students' memories, their imaginations, and their thinking and feeling about themselves now and in the future. We have attempted to appeal to their growing maturity rather than following trends or being cute.

The suggested exercises may be used in any manner or any order the teacher or the student desires. Perhaps an initial reading or skimming of the entire book would be helpful to gain an overview of the subject and the broad coverage the material offers. Certainly, teachers are encouraged to add their own ideas and exercises.

If time permits, a half hour a day might be set aside for journal writing. One hour on Friday afternoon or Monday morning might suit the classroom schedule. The teacher who desires a more spontaneous approach might fill in the bits and pieces of time that appear in a day unexpectedly. We encourage teachers to weave journal keeping in with other curriculum material. A unit on pioneers could certainly include reading pioneer diaries, writing about one's own ancestors, and writing creatively in a journal style, imagining life in those times. A unit on the future would be a good time for students to explore their own future. A relationship problem among students, or a personal experience of students, might trigger a journal entry by the whole class to explore feelings or do some problem solving. Many creative and sensitive teachers used the time of the *Challenger* disaster to allow students to write out feelings about the death of a loved one. Journal writing should never be allowed to become routine or pedantic. It should always be a special activity, approached with enthusiasm.

We will list books on journal technique that have helped us and offer bibliographies of journals and diaries that teachers and children alike will enjoy reading. We are both students of Tristine Rainer, whose book *The New Diary* is fast becoming a classic in the field. Barbara has taken the Progoff journal workshops designed by Ira Progoff, a leader in the journal field, and has taught journal keeping at the University of Colorado for ten years. Kathleen has taught many workshops on the subject. We have adapted all the techniques we have found inspiring to adults for teachers to use with children and teenagers. The examples we have included to show teachers and students what might be written as a result of an exercise are taken from old, published journals, or they are fiction. We have enjoyed writing some ourselves, perhaps dipping into our own memories or journals. We feel too strongly about the privacy of a child's journal to quote any real children's personal writing here.

We emphasize throughout the book that the material that comes from a young person's heart and mind and ends up in a journal is immensely private. Teachers must respect that privacy.

Why should journal exercises be a part of the school curriculum? Teachers are concerned with their students' whole education, their growth as individuals during the school year. The growing that children experience through personal writing will spill over into all aspects of school life. Even without sharing, journal writing together will draw a class closer together. We have seen this happen time after time in classes with adults in a caring and warm atmosphere. Just by giving a child the opportunity to do personal writing says, "I care about you. I want you to be a happy, worthwhile individual."

Progoff has said that each person's life is a work of art. The journal is a place to practice that art, to write oneself better and better. But also, it is a place to take a look at what is already painted and notice that a few brush strokes are needed here and there, not forgetting to appreciate that there are some really beautiful portions that are perfect the way they are. When artists paint, they step back and look, paint, step back and look. The journal is that place where one can step back, look at one's life as a whole, see how it's shaping up, and then add those polishing touches it needs.

Journal keeping is no panacea, no sure cure for what ails us personally, and, no, it is no passing, New Age fad. It is a tool that has worked for individuals for hundreds of years. Teaching young people the resources to draw on for in-depth journal keeping provides them with that valuable tool to use all their lives. They will get to know themselves better and find ways to become more creative and mature individuals. They will thank their teachers for this guidance the rest of their lives.

1

Why Keep a Journal?

Writing is a kind of double living. The writer experiences everything twice. Once in reality and once in that mirror.

—Catherine Drinker Bowen
Atlantic, December 1957

A PLACE TO PERSONALIZE HISTORY

Journal keeping may date back to the invention of paper. Journals were found in the ruins of Pompeii and in the tombs of Egypt. Many famous, creative people have kept journals. Among them are artist Leonardo da Vinci, novelist Fyodor Dostoyevski, diarist and public official Samuel Pepys; and women writers George Eliot, Louisa May Alcott, Virginia Woolf, and May Sarton.

One of the best-known women diarists is Anaïs Nin. Her five volumes are perhaps the most complete story of one woman's life ever published.

Everyone has heard of Jewish schoolgirl Anne Frank, who kept her diary while hiding from Nazi troops during World War II. And who has not read at least portions of *Walden*, taken from the journals of naturalist Henry David Thoreau?

For every famous person who has written and later published journals, there are thousands of unknown people throughout history who have recorded their everyday lives in writing. Sometimes portions of these records have been published documenting life in the early days of the United States, in the old West, on the Kansas frontier, in a Japanese relocation center in the United States during World War II, during the Civil War, and during the Great Depression.

What is gained from reading these journals rather than a history book, which gives us the same facts? History books do not give us feelings. Customs, technology, living conditions may change, but human emotions are the same whether you are living in Europe in the Middle Ages, in California during the Gold Rush, or in Colorado in the 1990s. It is both fascinating and comforting that the inner lives of other people are similar to our own.

A PLACE FOR SELF-DISCOVERY AND SELF-KNOWLEDGE

People today are rediscovering journal keeping as a means of self-discovery and self-knowledge. Children as well as adults can benefit from getting to know themselves better. They can enjoy recording the events of their lives. They can practice writing for the fun of it and exploring and playing with language with no fear that an adult will correct their spelling or grammar or punctuation.

I write, therefore I am.

—Samuel Johnson
Boswell's *Life of Dr. Johnson*

❑ ❑ ❑

A female prison inmate, after a course in journal keeping, said, "I feel like I have finally found myself. I got into drugs because I wouldn't accept all the hurt I grew up with." Perhaps journaling at an earlier age could have helped her understand herself and the people around her better. She may not have been able to avoid the hurt, but she could have written about it and perhaps gotten rid of it by putting her thoughts and feelings on paper. She would have had at least one friend she could trust.

A PERSONAL FRIEND AND A PLACE TO DOCUMENT YOUR LIFE

Many journalists refer to a diary as a friend, a friend who will always listen, one who will not criticize, and one who can keep a secret.

We live in a fast-paced world. A journal can help us slow down and enjoy our experiences or attempt to understand them. We are a society almost without solitude. Journaling can help us enjoy being alone and make us want to find time to spend alone.

Solitude is the school of genius.
—Edward Gibbon
*The History of the Decline
and Fall of the Roman Empire*

A recent study found that, contrary to popular opinion, an only child, with more time alone, is more independent and more sophisticated than a child with siblings; an only child is able to think on his or her own, and isn't easily swayed by peer pressure. The only child values being alone. Journal keeping can help an individual value his or her own life.

Ira Progoff, the father of modern journal keeping, believes that each person's life is his or her own great work of art. A journal documents that art.

Hughes Mearns, in his classic book, *Creative Power*, said to his students:

> Perhaps you have thought it just silliness, those thoughts and imaginings that roam about deep inside of you.... You have something to say. Something of your very own. Try to say it. Don't be ashamed of any real thought or feeling you have. Don't undervalue it. Don't let the fear of what others may think of it prevent you from saying it. Perhaps not aloud, but to yourself. You have something to say, something that no one else in the world has ever said in just your way of saying it....
>
> You have something to say, something important, but the thing itself is not half so important to you as what the saying will be to you. If you can teach yourself to find that unique and valuable possession inside of you and succeed in getting some of it out of you, you yourself will grow astonishingly in personal power. So search for it early. Get it started in order that you may begin to grow.*

---

*Mearns, Hughes. *Creative Power*. New York: Doubleday, Doran, 1930. P. 272.

A journal is the best place to do that searching, the best place to record those discoveries. A journal is a place where you will discover life.

We would like to encourage teachers to read and find interesting excerpts from the many diaries and journals that have been published. This will give the student examples of what others have written over the years. Certainly the students won't be expected to achieve such literary style, but will read them for content and inspiration. If the teacher keeps a journal, perhaps he or she could share an entry or two that is not too personal. We encourage teachers to continue or start their own journals and write along with their students.

POINTS TO REMEMBER

- People have been keeping journals since the invention of paper.

- Thoughts and feelings are universal. Reading other people's journals helps us realize that their lives were or are similar to our own.

- Journal keeping is a means of self-discovery and self-knowledge.

- Your journal is your best friend.

- A journal can help you enjoy being alone.

- A journal is a place where you will discover life.

- Your life is your own great work of art.

SUGGESTED READING

Students or teachers may browse through some of these books to find inspiration.

Books by Adults about Journal Keeping or Related Subjects

Benjamin, Carol Lea. *Writing for Kids.* New York: Harper & Row, 1985. Chapter on journals.

Capacchione, Lucia. *The Creative Journal.* Athens, Ohio: Swallow Press, Ohio University Press, 1979.

Casewit, Curtis W. *The Diary: A Complete Guide to Journal Writing.* Allen, Tex.: Argus Communications, 1982.

Hofmann, William J. *Life Writing: A Guide to Family Journals and Personal Memoirs.* New York: St. Martin's Press, 1982.

Jackson, Jacqueline. *Turn Not Pale, Beloved Snail.* Boston: Little, Brown, 1974. Chapter 10, "My Best Thoughts."

Jacobs, Gabriel H. L. *When Children Think: Using Journals to Encourage Creative Thinking.* New York: Teachers College Press, 1970.

Knott, Leonard. *Writing for the Joy of It.* Cincinnati: Writer's Digest Books, 1983.

Mearns, Hughes. *Creative Power.* Mineola, N.Y.: Dover, 1958.

_____. *Creative Youth.* New York: Doubleday, Page, 1927.

Ranier, Tristine. *The New Diary.* Los Angeles: J. P. Tarcher, 1978.

Rico, Gabriele Lusser. *Writing the Natural Way: Using Right-Brain Techniques to Release Your Expressive Powers.* Los Angeles: J. P. Tarcher, 1983.

Stillman, Peter R. *Families Writing.* Cincinnati: Writer's Digest Books, 1989.

Tchudi, Susan, and Stephen Tchudi. *The Young Writer's Handbook.* New York: Scribner, 1984. Chapter on journals.

Journals by Adults

Du Maurier, Daphne. *Myself When Young: The Shaping of a Writer.* New York: Doubleday, 1977.

Franklin, Penelope, ed. *Private Pages: Diaries of American Women 1830s-1970s.* New York: Ballantine, 1986.

Mallon, Thomas. *A Book of One's Own People and Their Diaries*. New York: Ticknor & Fields, 1984.

Moffat, Mary Jane, and Charlotte Painter, eds. *Revelations—Diaries of Women*. New York: Vintage, 1975.

Murry, J. Middleton, ed. *Journal of Katherine Mansfield*. New York: Ecco Press, 1983.

Sarton, May. *The House by the Sea*. New York: Norton, 1977.

_____. *Journal of a Solitude*. New York: Norton, 1973.

Naturalists' Journals

Many naturalists and wildlife biologists keep records, field notes, and observations in journal style. The following are three the authors have enjoyed. Combine a science study of the natural world around you with journal keeping. Encourage children to read passages of these books and then observe and write about the natural world around them in a like manner.

Dillard, Annie. *Pilgrim at Tinker Creek*. New York: Harper's Magazine Press, Harper & Row, 1974.

Leopold, Aldo. *A Sand County Almanac*. New York: Oxford University Press, 1968.

Woodin, Ann. *Home Is the Desert*. Tucson: University of Arizona Press, 1984.

Published Journals by Young People

Frank, Anne. *The Diary of a Young Girl*. New York: Scholastic, 1962.

Hoff, Benjamin, ed. *The Singing Creek Where the Willow Grows: The Rediscovered Diary of Opal Whiteley*. New York: Ticknor & Fields, 1986.

Whiteley, Opal. (Adapted by Jane Boulton) *Opal: The Journal of an Understanding Heart*. Palo Alto, Calif.: Tioga, 1984.

Yates, Elizabeth. *My Diary—My World*. Philadelphia: Westminster Press, 1981.

Fiction Written in Journal Style

Blos, Joan W. *A Gathering of Days: A New England Girl's Journal, 1830-32*. New York: Scribner, 1979.

George, Jean Craighead. *My Side of the Mountain*. New York: Dutton, 1959.

Glaser, Dianne. *The Diary of Trilby Frost*. New York: Holiday House, 1976.

Shute, H. A. *The Real Diary of a Real Boy*. Chicago: Reilly & Lee, no date.

CHAPTER 2

Techniques and Definitions

The art of the pen is to rouse the inward vision.
—George Meredith
Diana of the Crossways

Thus I set pen to paper with delight,
And quickly had my thoughts in black and white.
—John Bunyan
The Pilgrim's Progress

Many people have been surprised to learn that there are specific techniques for keeping a journal. Don't you just start writing about whatever is on your mind and ramble on and on until you run out of words? Certainly this is one technique, but only one, and it can severely limit the potential richness of journal keeping.

In this chapter we will discuss some ways and reasons for you and your students to keep a journal, and the classroom approach for using journals. You will notice that there are no *real* examples of children's writings here as there were in our past two books on children writing (*Creative Writing: A Handbook for Teaching Young People*, Libraries Unlimited, 1985, and *Catching Ideas*, Libraries Unlimited, 1988). The diary excerpts, except where documented, are fictitious examples; they are included to give an idea of expected results. They are written, however, in a free-form way (as a real journey-keeper would do), ignoring grammar, punctuation, and spelling rules.

JOURNAL OR DIARY?

Journal or diary: what shall we call it? *The New Random House Dictionary of the English Language* says:

diary: a daily record, usually private, esp. of the writer's own experiences, observations, feelings, attitudes, etc.

journal: a daily record, as of occurrences, experiences, or observations....

Many people use the terms interchangeably; to some, diary means appointment book or calendar; to some, a journal is a periodical or a bookkeeping notebook. Record book, daybook, writer's notebook, commonplace book, logbook, diary, journal—the word *journal* is the choice for this text. But journal keepers should be free to use whatever term feels right or strikes their fancy.

THE ACTUAL BOOK

What kind of book should you and your students choose for a journal? Well, you don't choose one of those little, five-cramped-lines-a-day books with a laughable excuse for a lock and key. Their predated pages alone are enough to discourage the most motivated of journal writers.

Many of us received one of those for Christmas when we were very young. It didn't take long for us to feel guilty that we weren't writing every day. Then when we did write, we felt obligated to go back and catch up, since there was a space for each day. Some days not enough happened to fill one line. Other days we could have filled five pages. We seldom kept past January 30 our New Year's resolution to write in a diary.

Books for journaling range from spiral notebooks with lined pages to blank-paged books bound in silk or leather. Some writers maintain that lined pages are restrictive, while others feel that beautifully bound volumes are too intimidating for beginners. One journal workshop teacher felt that her own young daughters were more inspired when they had beautiful books to work in. But for reasons of availability, economy, page-size, and familiarity, a spiral or bound composition book is probably the best choice for beginners.

Some people decorate their notebook covers with a picture that has special meaning for them or with a collage of pertinent illustrations.

One teacher encourages her children to label their books *The Secret Journal of (Suzy Jones or Bill Smith)*, the word *secret* meaning *private*. Then there are those who believe that a notebook that looks like any other, or is even labeled MATH or SOCIAL STUDIES, is less likely to be noticed, picked up, and read.

Encourage writers to use ink rather than pencil. Pencil not only smudges and is more difficult to read as time passes, but pencil is also too easily erased. Entries should remain as they were written, in the mood and with the feelings of that moment.

RULES/NO RULES

There are longtime journal keepers who quote many rules; there are others who insist that there should be no rules. Experience and practicality suggest these few.

Date every entry. Use month and date, and, at least on January 1, *the year.* Dating not only verifies when events actually happened, it also gives the writer an opportunity to see changes in thoughts, ideas, opinions, wishes.

Write legibly. Again, choose ink over pencil for readability and permanence. But don't worry about spelling, punctuation, or grammar. Here, it is the thought that is most important.

Be honest. Write fantasy if you want to. It is fine to use fact as a basis for fantasy, but don't let fact and fantasy become confused and mixed up together.

Keep your journal private. If you don't want others reading your journal without permission, don't flaunt it, don't talk about what you are writing in it, and don't leave it lying about. These are open invitations for others to read it.

An important "non-rule" is about what goes into a journal. Anything journal keepers want can go into a journal. They can use pictures, sketches, cartoons, or nothing but writing. They can write frontwards, backwards, or upside down. Leonardo da Vinci kept his notebooks in mirror writing. Samuel Pepys wrote his diary in a code that combined French, Spanish, Latin, Greek, a form of shorthand, and characters of his own invention. Although it shouldn't turn into just a scrapbook of mementos, a journal is indeed personal and should express the journalist's personal feelings.

OTHER SUGGESTIONS FOR JOURNAL KEEPERS

Value your writing. A journal is a record of a journey. Value what you have written. In rereading, you may find that some of your entries now sound silly or dumb. Don't throw them away or attempt to rewrite them. These entries represent steps along the way of your journey, steps that have helped you reach where you are today, where you will be tomorrow.

Write spontaneously. Most of the writing we do must be carefully thought out, put into proper grammatical form, with words spelled and sentences punctuated correctly. The journal is the place for free, unplanned writing, unhindered by shoulds and should nots.

Name your journal. Some people like to name each new journal as if it were a novel or perhaps a work of nonfiction: *My Best Year Yet* (you're so sure it will be, you name it beforehand); *My Fifth Grade Year*; *Life in Fourth Grade*; *Tales of a Fourth Grade Somebody*; *Sixth Grade Secrets*. Some just address the journal as they write, beginning "Dear Diary" or "Dear Me." But entries don't have to be like letters.

Vary writing forms. There are many ways to write in a journal:

- Monologues — you, explaining to or telling yourself

- Dialogues — discussions between two you's or between you and anyone you care to talk with

- Lists — lists of questions, statements, metaphors, or lists of words that represent people, ideas, wishes, plans

- Free intuitive writing — writing without thinking or planning

- Free intuitive drawing — drawing feelings or thoughts without a well-thought-out plan before you start, which could even take the form of doodles

- Character sketches or portraits — word pictures of people the writer likes or dislikes

Each of these suggestions will be presented in detail in the chapters that follow.

WHEN TO WRITE

Try to write for a few minutes every day. This is the time to pause and think about your own thoughts, to get acquainted with and visit with your friend, *You.*

If you don't write every day, don't feel guilty about it. Even the staid eleventh edition of the *Encyclopaedia Britannica* admits, "It is not necessary that the entries of a diary should be made each day, since every life, however full, must contain absolutely empty intervals." But if you're not writing in your journal regularly, think about reasons why.

- Are you lazy?

- Are too many of your days "absolutely empty intervals?" Maybe you need to stop, look, listen a little more to what is going on around you.

- Is there a repeated pattern to the days you don't want to or don't feel the need to write? Try to discover that pattern.

- Do you have trouble thinking of something to write about? This book will give you dozens and dozens of ideas to use as starters for journal writing.

Don't get so busy writing about your life that you forget to live it!

The very young heroine, Cecily, in Oscar Wilde's play *The Importance of Being Earnest* tells her governess, Miss Prism, about her diary,

Cecily: I keep a diary in order to enter the wonderful secrets of my life. If I didn't write them down I would probably forget all about them.

Prism: Memory, my dear Cecily, is the diary we all carry about with us.

Cecily: Yes, but it usually chronicles the things that have never happened and couldn't possibly have happened.

Of course, we remember many things that happen to us. And, of course, we forget as many more. But of those we remember, do we remember them as they really happened? So it follows that one reason for keeping a journal is to record the happenings and occurrences of our lives accurately.

REASONS TO KEEP A JOURNAL

To record actual happenings. Use your journal to write down in a simple fashion the events of your day.

ABC's Journal   March 1

Got up. Went to school. Won volleyball game after school. Came home. Watched TV.

A record such as this is little more than a basic logbook—just the facts.

An English navy clerk and member of Parliament who lived three hundred years ago was one of history's most famous diarists. Samuel Pepys (1633-1703) for several years recorded his London experiences and observations, giving today's readers a colorful picture of those times.

Pepys's Diary   26 January 1660

... my wife had got ready a very fine dinner: viz, a dish of marrow bones; a leg of mutton; a loin of veal; a dish of fowl; three pullets, and two dozen larks, all in a dish....

1 May 1663

Went to hear Mrs. Turner's daughter play on the harpsichon....

13 October 1660

I went out to Charing Cross, to see Major-General Harrison hanged, drawn, and quartered....

These are statements of fact. But Pepys's diary becomes more vivid and alive when we go on to read his comments about these facts.

Pepys's Diary   1 May 1663

Went to hear Mrs. Turner's daughter play on the harpsichon; but, Lord! it was enough to make any man sick to hear her, yet was I forced to commend her highly.

13 October 1660

I went out to Charing Cross, to see Major-General Harrison hanged, drawn, and quartered—which was done there—he looking as cheerful as any man could do in that condition.

By reading ABC's diary entry, it would be hard to distinguish March 1 from many other days in ABC's life. But ABC doesn't have to be a Samuel Pepys to bring March 1 back to mind and alive. All that is needed are a few personal remarks.

ABC's Journal   March 1

Well, I didn't oversleep this morning and neither did anyone else around here. Put my clock radio in my bottom dresser drawer so I wouldn't turn off the alarm in my sleep. Must have bumped the volume control because old Kibby Kibitzer on KKOK woke the whole family up before I could remember where I'd put my radio. Day went downhill fast from there on until our team finally won a volleyball game—even if it was by default because the other team never showed up....

To examine experiences, thoughts, ideas. Some journal keepers don't necessarily include the logbook facts in their entries. They are more interested in considering the whys and wherefores, the significance of their thoughts, ideas, and experiences.

ABC might use several pages in looking for reasons for oversleeping, or in exploring the family members' feelings about Kibby Kibitzer and Station KKOK, or in examining the problems of the volleyball team.

When writers use their journals to examine the things they are thinking about, they find that the writing becomes a way of talking to and with themselves.

To experiment with thoughts and ideas. Another way ABC might extend the journal's use beyond recording facts is to experiment with different kinds of writing.

ABC's Journal   March 1

In 1492 I overslept and missed the boat – the *Santa Maria.*

So – I stayed home and helped Queen Isabella get her jewelry back from the pawnshop.

In 1776 I overslept and missed signing the Declaration of Independence.

So – I went down to Kentucky and showed Daniel Boone how to build the Wilderness Trail.

In 2010 I overslept and missed the Monday shuttle to my job on the moon.

So – I stayed home and invented a time machine that gets me to work early no matter how late I sleep.

After interviewing family members, ABC might make this list of people's responses to the Kibby Kibitzer Show.

DAD	**MOM**	**CASSIE**	**ME**
Annoying	Awful	Adolescent	All right!
Blatting	Bragging	Birdbrained	Big!
Crazy	Crude	Childish	Clever!

REVIEW OF REASONS AND WAYS TO KEEP A JOURNAL: A BAKER'S DOZEN

To record

1. events
2. ideas, plans
3. thoughts, daydreams, secrets
4. feelings, emotions
5. ideas of others

To examine

6. events
7. ideas, plans
8. thoughts, daydreams, secrets
9. feelings, emotions
10. ideas of others

To experiment

11. by looking back and looking ahead
12. by playing with words and trying different kinds of writings
13. by finding ways to work out problems

THE JOURNAL IN THE CLASSROOM

Journal keeping in the classroom is an activity built on trust. A journal project must be optional, and certainly the sharing of journal entries must be optional. Students have to feel confident that no one will read their journals unless invited to. At the same time, they should know that they are welcome to share—with teacher or classmates—if they wish. And readers or listeners must always remember that being allowed to share someone's journal is a privilege and that they must never be judgmental.

Hughes Mearns in *Creative Power* says:

> If the creative life is to have its legitimate sustenance, it must be permitted at times to graze in its own private grounds. A confidence cannot be shouted to the crowd; and the first important creative activities of youth are confidential and confessional.*

Trust and confidence grow slowly. At first there might be a special drawer where journals or papers "for your own eyes only" could be left, inconspicuously, for teacher sharing. From there, a dialogue journal between teacher and pupil might grow, starting, perhaps, with just a sentence or question or two.

Sharing by reading aloud can develop confidence. When a writer is ready, he or she might first read to one person, then to a small group, and eventually to the class.

While there will never be any red penciling in journals (or any written comments, except in a dialogue journal), writers might be encouraged to develop a special sentence or paragraph into a brief essay, a poem, or even a story meant for sharing.

However, assigning journal entries for handing in, or publishing journal entries, turns the writing into something else. It is fiction, perhaps, or personal essay, but not journal. It is creating an artificial situation for artificial results. Great journalists have been published over the years, but as the work is shared with millions, it becomes other than journal. It becomes autobiography, a personal story.

---

*Mearns, Hughes. *Creative Power*. New York: Doubleday, Doran, 1930. P. 88.

Anne Frank never wrote in her diary for anyone except herself. She had no plan to share it. Probably it was published only because she did not survive her experience. But her personal thoughts did. Had she lived, she would no doubt have turned her diary into a story.

First and foremost, you, the teacher, must respect the privacy of your students. Until you do, they will be writing for the public eye, for someone other than themselves — you for starters. And reading a child's journal, or an adult's journal for that matter, without that person's permission, is no less a theft than taking personal possessions. You rob that person of something perhaps even more important and valuable — the freedom of private, personal thoughts.

POINTS TO REMEMBER

- A diary is a daily log.

- A journal records today, but also goes backwards or forward in time.

- The style of a journal is an individual choice.

- There are four suggested rules for journal keeping:
    Date each entry

    Write legibly

    Be honest

    Take the responsibility for keeping your journal private

- Value your own writing.

- Write spontaneously.

- Name your journal.

- Vary your writing forms.

- Write in your journal as often as possible.

- Reasons to keep a journal:
    To record actual happenings

    To examine experiences, thoughts, ideas

    To experiment with thoughts and ideas

- Sharing your journal is a personal choice.

CHAPTER 3

The Journal Records Today

He will through life be master of himself and a happy man who from day to day can have said, "I have lived."

—Horace
(65 B.C.)

INTRODUCTION

In 65 B.C. the philosopher Horace was telling people to live one day at a time in order to be happy. Many poets and philosophers have since quoted him or rephrased what he said. Psychologists are still reminding us that we will be happiest if we live for today alone. We cannot forget the past. We enjoy the anticipation of things we plan for the future. And certainly, just as we are a product of our past, what we do today will affect tomorrow. But today, now, is where our feet are resting. A journal can help us learn the joy of living in the present.

It is almost impossible, and probably not desirable, to write in a journal every day. But taking a few minutes at the end of each day to jot down events keeps us in touch with what is taking place inside ourselves. This is more of a log approach to journal keeping. One big advantage of logging in daily happenings is that it gives us material for in-depth writing when we have more time.

> *The present changes so quickly that we are not aware of our life at the moment of living it.*
>
> — George Moore
> *Ave*

There is certainly nothing wrong with living each day, each hour, to its fullest. Busy people are usually happy people. But you need some reminders so that you can write about your activities and feelings at a later date.

Let's say you made a long trip, came home late, and feel exhausted. You make a quick listing of your experiences with no description, no record of the feelings, even your enjoyment of the day. A few words may be enough to help you recall what you want to write about at length when time permits.

> Skied all day at Winter Park. Sun, snow bright, crisp.
> Velvet hot chocolate at top of mountain. Sam took a
> spectacular fall. Long drive home. I slept. We were all
> too tired to cook dinner. We ordered pizza.

In addition to logging in daily events, using the journal to explore today means finding out who we are as individuals right now, today. Yesterday we were someone else; tomorrow we will change again. We will look at ourselves to know ourselves better. "Know thyself" is a quotation ascribed to a number of famous philosophers. Who else can we really know and understand as well as ourselves? We can celebrate ourselves as individuals in the journal.

> *There is an unchanging silent life within every man that no one knows but himself.*
>
> — Anonymous

PURPOSES AND AIMS

- To promote awareness of living one day at a time

- To discover who we are today

- To look at what makes us individuals

- To give today a place in history, both as it relates to us personally and as it relates to the world around us

METAPHOR OF YOURSELF

Dramatist Edward Albee is quoted as saying that humans are the only animals who consciously create art, who use metaphor to understand themselves. As very young children, we have no trouble imagining that something is (like) something else, although we are very literal. As we grow older, we know that when a character in a Shakespeare play says, "Lend me your ears," he means only, "Listen to me." He isn't saying he needs two more ears.

But as young people and adults we have to be reminded that using metaphor and simile makes for good description. These figures of speech can help us picture something more clearly.

Think of a metaphor that describes your life right now. Using the power of metaphor will help you gain a creative and concise picture of yourself. For example, you might say, "I am a broken glass." This might suggest that right now you feel your life is broken into little pieces. You may feel it can never be put back together. You might say, "My life is a patchwork quilt, a jigsaw puzzle, a carousel horse, a golden butterfly, a secret garden, a spaceship." Remember that a metaphor compares two things. You are comparing your life to something else in order to see it better.

Be spontaneous. The first idea that comes to you may be closest to your feelings today. Tomorrow you might choose another. As soon as you have chosen your metaphor, discuss why you see your life this way.

> My life is a patchwork quilt. It is made up of tiny pieces of all my ancestors before me and me today.
>
> There is a rose-colored scrap that is my mother's cheery smile. My father says I have that same smile. There is a gray scrap from the uniform of my great uncle who was in the Confederate army. My mother says I get my stubbornness from him.
>
> A triangle of blue is sewn to a triangle of blue teddy bear print. When I started to school I took my teddy bear with me. I used to be very shy. Teddy-Jon helped me not feel so scared. I slept with him and carried him everywhere.
>
> There is a yellow patch with black musical notes on it. I like to play the piano, and I'm good at singing. Being in the school choir helps me be less shy now. My best friend is in the choir, too. She and I go everywhere together. I guess she is taking the place of

Teddy-Jon. She would laugh if I told her that. She laughs a lot. A big red patch is my best friend, Sara.

All these pieces are sewn together to make a quilt. This new quilt is me. And although I have taken pieces from a lot of places, the quilt forms a unique pattern that is my life. There are no other patchwork quilts like mine.

My life is a broken Christmas ornament. The day after Christmas this year, my life shattered into a thousand pieces. I don't think it can ever be glued back together. My father left home. I don't understand how someone I love can just disappear. My mother said it made him too sad to tell me he was leaving. Maybe he will come back when he can and talk to me. My parents are getting a divorce. Mother says we will have to move to an apartment. We won't be able to afford our house. She will try to find a place so I can go to the same school. If she can't, I will have to leave all my friends, too. I'm not the only one who is hurt by all the broken pieces. My mother cries a lot. I hear her at night. I hug my cat, Silky, and try not to listen. I wonder what will happen in the new year.

DRAWING YOURSELF

There is no rule that says a journal can't contain artwork. For some individuals, insight about oneself that won't come out in writing may be revealed through sketches or colored drawings.

Draw a picture of yourself right now—although not necessarily a photograph-like picture. You might draw the quilt metaphor you just wrote about. Perhaps you are a dancing car or a rolling ball of many colors. Your drawing might be totally abstract. It may be just a scribble of feelings. Or you might start to scribble and find the drawing takes a shape you hadn't expected. Whether you are writing or drawing, always think of this as a time to discover yourself.

Draw your life as a pie. Illustrate each slice as a piece of your whole life. The slices may not be all the same size.

INTRODUCING YOURSELF

What if you needed to tell a stranger all about yourself? Write an imaginary letter to a new pen pal introducing yourself. Make yourself sound like a person this new pal would want to correspond with, but be honest. You will seem more human to your new friend if you reveal some of your weaknesses. No one wants a friend, even a pen pal, who is perfect.

Write a letter to one of your ancestors telling how you turned out or thanking him or her for the traits passed down to you through the generations.

YOUR NAME

A person's name is very individual. It is an important part of who you are. Find out where your name came from. Is it a family name? Was it a popular name at the time you were born? Is it a name from the Bible or from other literature? Does the name suggest a period of history or a place? Your heritage? Why did your parents choose this name for you? Do you like or dislike your name? Do you think your name suits you? Why? What does your name mean?

- Write a piece about your name.

- Make a list of nicknames you've had or have. Who gave you this nickname? Why? Does it suit you?

- If you could choose another name for yourself, what would it be? Why? A nickname?

- Write or print your name in larger letters. Draw a picture around your name that helps describe you.

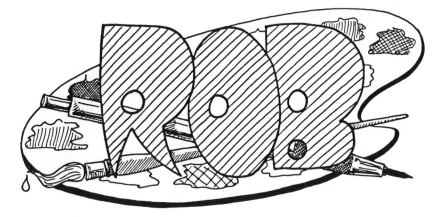

CHARACTER TRAITS

Over the years you have developed many personal character traits. Perhaps you inherited some of them, but some are uniquely your own. Some you may like, and some you may dislike and need to work on. By looking at them, you will discover more about yourself. Explore your traits by answering these questions one by one:

- List ten words that describe you best.

- Rank them one through ten, the best or most descriptive of you being number one.

- What is your main character trait? Discuss it.

- What is your strongest positive trait?

- What trait gets you in the most trouble? Why is this?

- Does this same trait sometimes get you out of trouble, or does it get you things you want? For example, stubbornness may cause you many problems with your family and friends, but it may also help you reach goals.

- What trait do you most admire in friends? This is probably a trait you would like to have. How could you go about including it in your personality?

> *What lies behind us and what lies before us are small matters to what lies within us.*
>
> —Ralph Waldo Emerson

YOU ARE MANY PEOPLE

All of us are made up of many individuals, or, put another way, we play many roles. If we said, "Will the real you please stand up," several people would stand. We are different people for different situations. You are a different person at school than you are at home. Out with your friends or on a date, you may be yet another person. You may act differently around the opposite sex. You may be a very different person when you are with your grandmother than when you are with your mother.

Because of this fact, however, we may start to wonder who we really are. We may start to feel like a jigsaw puzzle that someone forgot to put together.

By identifying the individuals who make up your whole, you can acknowledge each of them, see what part each plays in your life, and call on one or more when you need them. There are times when a group is stronger than an individual, when a committee can make decisions better than a single person.

The people inside you have a lot in common with each other. They have the same history. They inhabit the same physical body. They have the same ancestors, the same family members.

You will be a much stronger individual if you can get your committee to work together rather than at odds. This is the main purpose of identifying your members. And sometimes there is one member who is terribly quarrelsome or hard to get along with. You may have to discipline this member or even throw him or her out of the committee.

Make a list of the people who make up your committee.

Dreamer	Optimist
Leader	Stubborn Self
Artist	Nice Self
Scaredy-Cat	Cold-Water-Dasher

Are there any people you used to be or that you have thrown out of your committee?

Now, think of something that is bothering you, a decision you need to make, a person you want to meet, something you want or need to do, something you want or need to change. Have a committee meeting and discuss what you can do about the situation. When you have finished, go back and see who spoke most often. Is this usual? Good? Did anyone get out of hand? Who seemed to have the best ideas? Who was most reasonable? Do you need to dialogue with one of your selves who is giving you trouble?

Leader:	We're here today to discuss meeting the new boy who's in math and English class.
Dreamer:	I'd sure like to meet him. I can just see myself going to a movie or even the next dance with him.
Scaredy-Cat:	I could never go up to him and say, "Hi, my name is Cindy. Would you like to be my friend?"
Leader:	Maybe that's not the approach to take anyway. But remember that everything scares you.
Optimist:	He might like to meet us. He may need some friends. After all, he is new in our school. He might be really happy if we introduced ourselves.
Cold-Water-Dasher:	This is a really dumb idea. He won't like us. He'll think we're silly.
Leader:	You're putting yourself down again. How do you know he won't like us? And it's certainly not a dumb idea. Making new friends is never dumb.
Nice Self:	It would be the nice thing to do. Think if you were new at a school.
Cold-Water-Dasher:	Nicey-wicey. Think how terrible you'll feel when he just stares at you and walks away.
Optimist:	He wouldn't do that. He looks like a nice guy.
Dreamer:	He's my ideal guy. I have this picture in my mind of a guy like him with curly brown hair and blue eyes and we'll go to a movie and he'll say he always wanted to meet a girl like me and he'll ask me to go steady and....
Leader:	I think you're carrying this a bit too far. All we want to do is meet him. We might not even like him. But we can be friendly.
Stubborn Self:	I'm going to get us a date for the next dance if it kills me. I say we do something.
Cold-Water-Dasher:	He may already have a date for the dance.
Nice Self:	Then he'll say he does, but he'd like to get to know us anyway.
Leader:	What if we had some plan other than a date?

Dreamer:	Like asking him to help you with your math and then he'd come over and he'd like studying together and he'd want to come over every day and he'd love the cookies your mother makes and you'd find out his mother is dead and he's lonely and....
Scaredy-Cat:	Good grief! You can't stay in the real world more than two minutes can you? But I'd be nervous if he came to the house and I had to be alone with him.
Artist:	Could I say something?
Leader:	Certainly. You're being awfully quiet.
Artist:	What if we got on the committee to decorate for the dance? Then we go up to him and say we need help, that we especially need guys to climb up and hang crepe paper, or that we heard he was artistic and we need more ideas.
Cold-Water Dasher:	Don't act so silly. We can climb up and hang crepe paper.
Artist:	Of course we can. We could do without him. But wasn't this whole meeting to decide what we could do to meet him?
Leader:	It certainly was. I think getting him on the decorating committee is a great idea. We could get to know him and see if we liked him. He would feel needed and could make some new friends. It would be time together that wouldn't be scary since we'd all be working. And he wouldn't think we were chasing after him. There would be a lot of people around, so it wouldn't make us nervous to be around him like it would if we were alone. This sounds like a good solution. All in favor?
Committee:	Aye.

PEOPLE IN YOUR LIFE TODAY

No one is alone in the world. There are people around you: people you live with, people who are your friends, people who are your enemies, people who teach and help you. Make a list of the important people in your life. Whom do you consider the most important other person in your life? Why? What people nurture, influence you? How and why? Perhaps there is an animal in your life that nurtures you.

My teacher says something that nurtures me means it feeds me, but not like food. It feeds my soul or mind or feelings. And I feel better afterwards. My cat nurtures me. When something bad happens to me or I get my feelings hurt, I can hold Scooter and he purrs. I know he loves me no matter what I do. And there's something about him being all warm and furry that makes me feel all warm and fuzzy inside. He squints his eyes and smiles at me and bumps my chin with his head. It's like he gobbles up my bad feelings and scratches them to bits. Because soon they're all gone. I read that old people feel better when they hold a cat or a dog. I understand this. What do people do who don't have a cat to hug?

What things in your life nurture you? What places in your life nurture you?

This is my secret place where I go to leave my bad feelings behind. There are a lot of bushes in our backyard. I can crawl way up underneath one of them. Some branches hang down, so no one can see me easily. I curl up there and hug my knees up to my chin and let the world go on without me. It's like a place I can hide or rest from everybody. When my mother and father fight, I run and crawl under there. I can't hear them. I can only hear the rustling of a field mouse or a bug in the leaves. I can only see tiny green leaves in rows on each branch and some ants who come by. I can smell the earth and dry leaves. I stay there until the lump in my throat goes away and I know I'm not going to cry. Or until I cry, but no one sees me. I stay until I get warm inside again. Sometimes I take my doll, Rachel, with me. No one else knows about this place.

Who is your best friend? Why? Describe your relationship. What trait do you admire most in him or her? Describe yourself the way you imagine your best friend would describe you. Why does he or she like you? What does he or she admire in you?

LOGGING IN DAILY EVENTS

If you were captain of a ship, every day you would log in what happened. You are captain of your life, so each day, at the end of the day, take a few minutes to write down the day's events. If you miss a day, don't worry, but writing down a few words or a paragraph can get to be a habit, and you will enjoy reading the daily events later. Use these partial sentences to help you think over the day.

Today I did ...

Today I felt ...

Today I felt bad about ...

Today I felt happy about ...

What I liked best about today was ...

The good things that happened today were ...

THE CURRENT EVENTS JOURNAL

Over the years we have learned a lot about history from people's journals. We know what life was like for the pioneers from men and women who wrote about their daily lives and what was happening around them. We know how ordinary people felt about historic events.

What do you consider the most interesting or important or unusual event that happened today outside your own life? Detail the event, discuss how you feel about it, and give your personal opinion of what it means to you or to the world. You might even include a newspaper clipping in your journal.

Today the emperor of Japan was buried. He was ruler of Japan during World War II. Some people thought he should have been tried as a war criminal. I think he realized the mistakes he made and was glad to live out the rest of his life in peace.

Today people started tearing down the Berlin Wall. The people who lived behind the wall were not free. Now they can decide for themselves where they want to live, what work they want to do, and who they want to lead their country. I hope this is the beginning of the whole world living together in peace.

Draw a graph of today using circles. The center circle is the most important thing that happened to you today. The next circle is what happened in your town. The next circle is what happened in your state. The fourth circle is the most important thing that happened in the United States. The last circle is the most important thing that happened in the world today.

Discuss these things as a whole. Did what happened in the world (your town, state, United States) have any effect on your life today?

Today President Truman announced that World War II was over. Our whole neighborhood was excited. James Valentine's father told all us kids we could get into the back of his truck. There were twelve of us. We drove downtown. Lots of people were doing the same thing. Cars and trucks and bicycles made a spontaneous parade that rolled slowly down Broadway. We yelled and screamed and banged on the side of the truck until we were hoarse. James had brought some money from his bank. We went to King Kone where he treated for ice cream. Counting his mother and father, it cost him a dollar and forty cents! My brother just graduated from high school. He's going to join the navy, but I'm glad he won't have to fight in the war.

Writing down current events will be especially fun to do on your birthday. Get in the habit of doing it every birthday. Some people like to get a copy of the newspaper that came out the day they were born. Could you do some research to find out what happened on your birthday date in other years? When you get older you will enjoy reading about the events that happened in the world during your lifetime.

CONCLUSION

By finding out about yourself, you can soon decide what is really important to you. You can learn to follow a path that is true to your nature. It will be easier to stand up to people and events outside you, to say, "I like who I am."

> *Nothing is more sacred than the laws of our own nature,*
> *and we must thoroughly look within ourselves and not*
> *permit outside standards to be imposed upon us.*

> — Ralph Waldo Emerson

◲   ◲   ◲

You will always be changing. You will be improving on your life, your personality. You will add new friends, learn new skills, gain ability to do things better. The person you are today will not be the same person a year from now, or even next week. But the more you study yourself, the more you will appreciate the unique individual you are.

POINTS TO REMEMBER

- A journal helps you learn the joy of living in the present.

- A journal helps you discover the individual you are today.

- Metaphor can help you gain a creative and concise picture of yourself.

- Spontaneous drawing can help you see yourself.

- You are made up of many people. Discover each one's role in your life.

- Getting to know the important people in your life will tell you much about yourself.

- You have a place in history. Use your journal to relate to the rest of the world.

- Follow a path that is true to your nature.

SUGGESTED READING

The following are some books about developing a sense of self.

Baker, Jill. *Basil of Bywater Hollow.* New York: Henry Holt, 1987. Basil thinks of himself as nothing but a big clumsy bear until disaster strikes the fair and his actions save the day.

Barrett, Joyce Durham. *Willie's Not the Hugging Kind.* New York: Harper & Row, 1989. When someone makes fun of Willie for hugging, he stops, but then he finds he gets lonely and unhappy.

Capacchione, Lucia. *The Creative Journal for Children: A Guide for Parents, Teachers and Counselors.* Boston: Shambhala, 1982. Distributed by Random House, 1989. Self-perception.

Cazet, Denys. *Great-uncle Felix.* New York: Orchard, 1988. A young boy gains self-confidence, love, and the value of memory from his great-uncle.

Clifton, Lucille. *Sonora Beautiful.* New York: Dutton, 1981. A Skinny Book. Sonora learns to accept herself, her name, and her heritage. For older readers with limited reading skills.

Corbin, William. *A Dog Worth Stealing.* New York: Orchard, 1987. Finding a dog, being responsible for it, and caring for it gives a child self-confidence.

Damjan, Mischa. *The Fake Flamingos.* New York: North-South Books, 1987. Unhappy with being a stork, Click persuades her husband, Clack, that they should become flamingos.

Gauch, Patricia Lee. *Christina Katerina and the Time She Quit the Family.* New York: Putnam, 1987. When CK quits the family, she finds she is lonely on her own.

Gilbert, Sara D. *By Yourself.* New York: Lothrop, Lee & Shepard, 1983. A latchkey child finds the confidence to be alone.

Hoffman, Mary. *Nancy No-size.* New York: Oxford University Press, 1987. Nancy suddenly finds she is neither short enough or tall enough, but as middle member of the family she discovers she is special in her own way.

Howe, James. *I Wish I Were a Butterfly.* New York: Gulliver, 1987. A wise spider helps a despondent cricket realize that he is special in his own way.

Mendez, Phil. *The Black Snowman.* New York: Scholastic, 1989. When a Kente helps a child build a black snowman, she finds pride in her African heritage.

Mills, Claudia. *Cally's Enterprise.* New York: Macmillan, 1988. When Cally meets everyone's expectations except her own, she finds she is not happy.

Nobens, C. A. *Shy Charlene and Sharyl.* New York: Little, Brown, 1987. Charlene uses a puppet to gain self-confidence.

Wegscheider-Cruse, Sharon. *Learning to Love Yourself: Finding Your Self Worth.* New York: Health Communications, 1987.

The Journal Remembers the Past

Underneath the surface of Today,
Lies Yesterday....

—Eugene Lee-Hamilton
"Roman Baths"

INTRODUCTION

In our journals we record today and the present — and that present quickly becomes yesterday and the past. The journal can also be a place to record today's memories of the past. How we see either today or yesterday will be colored and influenced by the memories, feelings, and experiences out of our past. Anaïs Nin called memory "a great betrayer," saying that when she read her diary she found it different from the way she had remembered scenes and conversations. But a nineteenth-century historian, J. A. Proude, seemed to feel it reasonable to remember with less than absolute accuracy. "We read the past," he said, "by the light of the present, and the forms vary as the shadows fall, or as the point of vision alters."

Whether most of our memories are precisely accurate or slightly blurred by time is not, usually, of as much importance as how we remember them. Going back to the past must not be done in a critical or judgmental way. Rather than thinking, I shouldn't have done that or I wish I'd done things differently, it is best to look at the past as the place where I was then — a necessary part of the progress to where I am now.

Remembering what was important to us in earlier days can help us understand what seems important — or unimportant — to us today. We can better understand where we are today by occasionally looking back and considering our yesterdays.

PURPOSES AND AIMS

- To recall and appreciate our own past

- To learn about and appreciate our family's past

- To see ourselves in relation to the world around us

- To understand ourselves better today by seeing where we have been

THE EARLIEST MEMORY AND WRITING ABOUT IT

What is your earliest memory? Is this the first time you've tried to recall it? How far back can you go? Is your earliest memory of your very first day of school? An early birthday, Christmas, or Hanukkah? Does it involve other people? An animal? A place, visit, or trip? Are you sure that this is your own memory and not a family anecdote you've heard so many times you feel as if you were remembering it yourself?

When you decide on that earliest memory, do you see it as a picture or a photograph? Or does it have action so that as you remember, you see the incident as if it were a movie?

If you're not sure which of your early memories is the first one, try making a list. This could be a general list:

- My first day of kindergarten
- The birthday I got Rover
- My first haircut
- A visit from my grandmother

Or you might make a list of specific early memories:

- People

    kindergarten teacher

    Grandma

    barber

- Animals

    Rover as a puppy

    elephants at zoo

- Places

    Lincoln Elementary School

    first house I lived in

    somebody's (whose?) sandbox

Other early memories might be of a trip or visit, an event or happening, an object, or an idea, belief, or wish.

Choose from your list the memory you believe to be your earliest and write it out as you remember it. For example: I remember my grandmother showing my brothers and me picture postcards from a trip she'd just made.

Now search your memory for more details and, using those details and thinking about the way you visualize your memory, write another paragraph.

> My brothers and I were ready for bed. We ran into my grandmother's room. She was tired from her trip, and she was ready for bed, too. We jumped up onto her bed so she could show us her pictures. The light over her bed was bright, and everything it was shining on seemed white—my grandmother's robe, my nightgown, my brothers' pajamas, and the spread over the bed. The rest of the room was dark. I see the picture as it is happening, but I am also in it, feeling happy and excited because I don't have to go to bed just yet.

Do other members of your family or your friends remember this incident? How do their memories differ from yours?

Friend: Yes, I remember the birthday you got Rover. He ate my ice cream and he popped my balloon.

Mother: Yes, I remember that birthday and that party—but I'm sure it was an angel food cake and not a chocolate one.

WALKING BACKWARDS

Instead of trying to reach back for the very earliest memory, experiment with going back a little at a time. Choose a yearly event (holiday, birthday, first or last day of school, or such) and think of something special about each one. List people you especially remember for each year. Or decide on the most memorable happening during each year. Start with this year or last year and walk back in your memories, one year at a time.

Searching as you walk. Make lists or write a few sentences about each of the first days of school that you can remember.

What were the subjects you liked best or least each year?

Does your remembering or thinking about these things make you think of certain people you knew during each school year? List all of your school teachers, then, for each year, list another person at school whom you remember something special about. List something special about each school year.

I remember that the year I was in fourth grade the book I liked best was *The Borrowers*. In third grade Miss Pettijohn read us *Charlotte's Web*. When I was in second grade I read *Ferdinand* every week, and in first grade I liked *Where the Wild Things Are* best.

Starting with this year or last year, write something special that you did or that you remember about each of the following holidays:

- New Year's Day
- Valentine's Day
- Fourth of July
- Halloween
- Thanksgiving

Halloween: When I was in fourth grade I was a witch. When I was in third grade I went as a refrigerator, second grade I was a clown, first grade I was a tiger, and kindergarten I was a cowboy. Before that I had to be a lamb because my big sister was Mary as in had a little lamb.

List the best-remembered gifts you received for each Christmas, birthday, or other special event. Then list the best gifts you gave in each year that you can recall.

Best Happenings

When I was nine — trip to Disney World

        eight — brand new bike

        seven— won boys' high jump, Field Day

        six   — best friend moved next door

        five   — started kindergarten

        four — new baby sister

        three — ?

        two   — ?

        one   — ?

        zero — I was born (I'm fooling. I don't remember that.)

Writing about what you've found. Choose a memory you've recorded and examine it. Look for details, reasons, and feelings.

> I remember how when I was in fourth grade I made up my mind I was going to fool everybody with my costume. I decided to be a Halloween witch. My mother made me a black witch's hat and a long black dress. I made a wig with long gray hair out of strips of newspaper that we curled with a knife blade, and I wore a red devil's mask. I sneaked the long way round so no one would know which way I came to school. And no one could guess who I was because they thought anyone dressed up like a witch would have to be a girl.

> I remember that the book I liked best in third grade was *Charlotte's Web.* As soon as Miss Pettijohn finished reading it to us, I got it from the library and read it again. Both times I cried when Charlotte died.

> When I was in kindergarten my mother gave me *Where the Wild Things Are* because she got tired of bringing it home from the library for me.

Does "Walking Backwards" help you remember more early memories? Does remembering certain people help you remember special happenings? Does remembering a certain teacher help you recall books you read, field trips you took, and school programs during that year?

Now, after going back and remembering these people and happenings, have you found an even earlier first memory?

REMEMBERING PEOPLE

Perhaps you wrote about people you had known in school when you were "Walking Backwards." Now think about some of the people you have known outside of school, people you haven't seen for a long time.

- Neighbors

    grown-ups and children

- Teachers and coaches

    music

    sports

    dance or drama

    Sunday school

- Family friends

- People at work

    doctor, dentist, veterinarian

    rabbi, priest, minister

    school bus drivers

    store clerks

Or what about people you remember but never really knew? Maybe there was a woman who seemed always to be working in her garden as you went by on your way to school, or a three-year-old who used to wave to you as you walked by his house. Did the letter carrier in your neighborhood say hello and call you by name, even though you never knew hers? There might be people you feel you know but never could have met in person—ancestors or long-gone friends you've heard about in family stories.

After you've listed (on paper or in your mind) some of these people you no longer see or never saw, choose one to make a word picture of. Or you might tell something about that person—what he or she did, an anecdote, or a special memory. Think about why you remember that person.

Try putting down in dialogue:

- A conversation you had with that person,

- A conversation you imagine having had with that person,

- A conversation you might have with that person if you could see him or her today.

REMEMBERING EVENTS

Personal events. In the "Walking Backwards" exercise you might have listed the best events you could remember in past years. What other events stand out in your memory? If you can't think of anything, go fishing. That doesn't necessarily mean that you should get your rod and bait and head for the nearest creek or river, although that might help, too. This kind of fishing is in the stream of your memory with words as fishhooks.

I remember

    my first/last _____

    the first time I _____

    the last time I _____

    the best _____

    the worst _____

    the funniest/silliest _____

    the happiest _____

    the scariest _____

    the first movie I remember going to was _____

    the worst day I ever had was _____

    the scariest book I ever read was _____

After you have finished several of the above sentences or some of your own, choose one to write about in detail.

> I remember the first time I went to the library by myself. I checked out one book. It was *Frog and Toad Are Friends.* By the time I got home I had read it all the way through. I read it again. The next day I went back to the library by myself and I forgot my card. The lady at the desk asked me my name and address and looked at her computer and said I could take my books anyway. That time I checked out four books and they lasted me for two days. My mother said maybe I should just move to the library.

If you recall an event but not the details, ask yourself questions: Who? What? When? Where? Why? How?

My best birthday present:

    Who (gave it to me)? Mom and Dad

    What? Rover

    When? My fifth birthday, right after breakfast

    Where? Backyard

    Why? Birthday present

    How? He was in a basket with a ribbon on the handle. He was asleep until I yelled, "A PUPPY!"

The Best Thing That Happened to Me Last Year

Who? Me

What? Got elected homeroom president

When? Fifth grade, spring term

Where? Lincoln School

Why? Because I had the best election campaign

How? I bought two packages of pencils and put stick-em notes on them and gave them to all the kids in my room. The notes said USE THIS PENCIL TO VOTE FOR MIKE!

But in recalling and writing about things that have happened to you, remember that journals are not like those sundials that are inscribed *I count only the sunny hours.* Journals are for writing about bad times as well as good ones, about losing as well as winning.

Events that happened to others. The happenings you write about don't all have to be your own. You can write of things that happened to people you know or events you have read about in newspapers or magazines or that you have heard about.

I remember hearing my grandfather tell about _____

I remember watching television the day that _____

I remember the day the boy next door _____

Do events that have happened to you remind you of events that have happened to people you know or that have happened to characters in books or stories you have read or plays you have watched? Do events in plays or books remind you of things that have happened to you?

When I read *The Incredible Journey* I thought about the summer our cat Reddy left home. He went away at the beginning of June and he was gone all summer long. So finally we gave up and we got a new kitten. On the day school started in September Reddy meowed at the front door. We let him in and he looked bigger and blacker than ever so he certainly hadn't gone hungry all summer. We were glad to have him home but when he saw that little kitten he was so mad he stomped and growled all over the place and he wouldn't go outside again for about two weeks.

Why do you suppose you remember the people or places or happenings that you do? Do any of your friends or family members remember these things? Choose one or more people to ask. Do they remember the incident or person or place the same way you do? If not, why do you suppose your memories differ?

Pretend that someone, real or imaginary, shared a happening with you. Write about what that person might be remembering.

REMEMBERING PERSONAL BELIEFS, IDEAS, OR WISHES

Think back over things you used to wonder about or believed or wished were so. Make some lists, then choose one or two to write about. Completing the following sentences may help you remember.

I used to believe _____

Because someone (friend, big brother, baby-sitter, etc.) told me, I believed that _____

Kids at school said _____

I used to wonder why/how _____

Grownups told me _____

I used to be afraid of _____

I did not believe _____

I still believe (or would like to believe) _____

I used to (or still) wish that _____

Because my big brother said so, I used to believe that the way you could tell that a cat was a tomcat was by looking at the way the fur grew in front of his ears.

Kids at school said if you jumped rope one hundred times without stopping you'd drop dead. I didn't believe it but I never had a chance to find out because I couldn't jump one hundred times without missing.

REMEMBERING YOUR FAMILY

O Damsel Dorothy! Dorothy Q.!
Strange is the gift that I owe to you, ...
Such a gift as never a king
Save to a daughter or son might bring ...
What if a hundred years ago
Those close-shut lips had answered No ...
Should I be I, or would it be
One tenth another, to nine tenths me?

—Oliver Wendell Holmes
"Dorothy Q.—A Family Portrait"

In his poem "Dorothy Q." Oliver Wendell Holmes wondered who he might have been had his great-grandmother, a hundred years before, said no instead of yes, had she not married the person she did.

If your family has stories and family records that go back many years, you might be interested in finding out about your ancestors. But even if you don't choose to go back years and years into family history, there are many other things to look into and write about.

Names. Why were you given your name? Is it a traditional name in your family? If so, who else has had it?

Do you have nicknames? How did you get them? Do others in your family have nicknames?

What is the history of your last name—its national origin, meaning, changes in spelling?

Traditions. Do your family members celebrate certain holidays? Do you have special customs for these holidays?

Does your family have special customs or traditions, either serious ones or ones that are observed for fun? What are their origins and histories?

Does your family have special games you play on certain occasions? Do you play games that your family has made up?

Do you have family reunions? Does your own family get together with relatives for holidays?

Have you heard stories from your relatives about grandparents, great-uncles or aunts, or more distant relatives?

Does your family have keepsakes or heirlooms handed down from earlier times? Are any of them children's toys? Do you know stories about these keepsakes?

Does your family have and use recipes from other generations? Do you know or can you find out their histories?

> I've been thinking about Valentine's Day and I guess it's more important to our family than it is to most folks. For a long time I thought everybody celebrated it the way we do, but then I found out lots of folks don't even notice February 14. When we moved here we came on Valentine's Day so that makes it double-special for us. We have an extra nice dinner Valentine's evening and Mother always has a pink decorated cake for us. Daddy brings flowers and candy for Mom but we all get to eat the candy. We all give each other valentines and Mom and Daddy have been sending the very same valentine back and forth to each other since before they got married. Next to Christmas and birthdays, I guess Valentine's Day is our favorite holiday.

Today I was looking at an old, old cookbook that belonged to my great-great-grandmother. It is so old that the pages are yellow-brown and the corners of them are breaking off. I found this recipe for angel food cake: "One and a half glasses of sugar, a good full glass of sifted flour, sift flour and sugar together five times, beat the white of twelve large or thirteen small eggs and a pinch of salt for a little while, then add half a teaspoon of cream tartar, finish beating, add small teaspoon vanilla, dump in the flour and sugar, mix with hand, have only a little heat in oven, bake one and a half hours."

Photographs. Does your family have photograph albums or collections of pictures? Are they recent, old, very old, or a combination? Are they labeled? If not, or without looking at the information, what could you guess about the people in the pictures? Look for details of facial expressions, clothing, and backgrounds. What was or what do you think was the occasion for taking the picture? Who do you suppose took the picture? In looking over old family pictures, do you see family resemblances?

Start a family album with word pictures of some of your ancestors and more immediate relatives. Write about your own feelings as you look at family pictures the way Oliver Wendell Holmes wondered about his great-grandmother when he looked at her picture.

Today I found a picture of Mom and Daddy's wedding. In the picture Mom looks just like Dorie but Mom says then she was four years older than Dorie is. Twenty and sixteen. Daddy sort of looks like he does now except he's in a navy officer's uniform. I asked Mom about her wedding and she told me about her wedding gown and the music and flowers and wedding cake. It must have been a good party because she and Daddy look so happy and laughing in the picture. And I had the craziest feeling about it. I didn't tell Mom but all of a sudden I felt kind of jealous and hurt and left out because I hadn't been there too. How dumb can you get!

See Suggested Reading section at the end of this chapter for books about writing family stories, histories, and memoirs, and ways of writing about them.

TIME LINES

You and history. What *other* important events happened on the date you were born? What was going on around the world the year you were born? What happened exactly one, ten, fifty, one hundred years ago on your birthday? Do you share your birthday with people you know, or with well-known or famous people of the past or present?

At the library you can find reference books that will give you time-line information. Several of these books are listed in the Suggested Reading section at the end of this chapter. Year-end news magazines and newspapers list the year's important international, national, and local events, and some newspapers carry a daily column listing the important events and birthdays for that date, going back one hundred years and more. Libraries will have both local and national newspapers on file, and some gift and novelty companies will reproduce front page copies of well-known newspapers for specific dates.

Using whatever research material you can, create a time line for your own birth date, going into the distant or recent past. (The illustration goes only to 1913.) Bring it up to date if you like, showing important happenings for each year of your life. Do you remember any of these events? Did any of them, directly or indirectly, affect you?

JANUARY 1

Abraham Lincoln signed
the Emancipation Proclamation

First Rose Bowl
football game*

U.S. Parcel Post
service began

1735   1863   1895   1902   1913

Paul Revere
was born

J. Edgar Hoover
was born

*University of Michigan
defeated Stanford University
49-0.

A personal time line. In using your journal to examine your past, you have gone back into your own history looking for your earliest, happiest, scariest, and funniest memories. You've thought about people you've known, events that have been important to you, and beliefs, ideas, and wishes you've held. Now you have material to make your own personal time line. Some journal keepers call this kind of list stepping-stones, a path, or milestones. You might see it as a ladder, stair steps, or even as building blocks.

Earlier you may have made lists of the best, worst, or silliest thing that happened to you each year. In your time line, stepping-stones, or personal ladder you will be putting down the most *important* things that have happened to you (see illustration of a personal time line). These will include unhappy events as well as happy ones. There may be more than one event in one year, and there may be several years when nothing of major importance seemed to happen. After you have labeled some of your stepping-stones or ladder rungs, you might want to add how you felt at those times. You also might want to try combining personal and historic time lines.

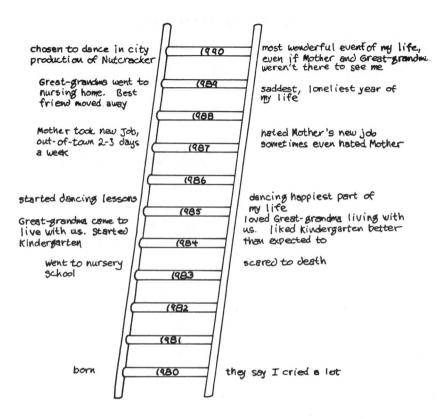

chosen to dance in city production of Nutcracker

1990

most wonderful event of my life, even if Mother and Great-grandma. weren't there to see me

Great-grandma went to nursing home. Best friend moved away

1989

saddest, loneliest year of my life

1988

Mother took new Job, out-of-town 2-3 days a week

1987

hated Mother's new job sometimes even hated Mother

1986

started dancing lessons

1985

dancing happiest part of my life
loved Great-grandma living with us. liked kindergarten better than expected to

Great-grandma came to live with us. Started Kindergarten

1984

went to nursery school

1983

scared to death

1982

1981

born

1980

they say I cried a lot

CONCLUSION

Pausing to look back now and then gives us time to think about where we've been. How accurately we remember is of less importance than how we feel about what we remember. The shadows fall differently for different people, the point of vision alters with time and distance. Still, memories of what we have experienced help us to understand where we have been, where we are now, and, perhaps, even where we may be going.

POINTS TO REMEMBER

- The journal is a place to record your memories of the past.

- "The Present is the living sum-total of the whole Past" (from Thomas Carlyle's *Essays: Characteristics*)

- Consider yesterday, appreciate it, but do not mourn or criticize it. Do not wish for it to be today.

- In "Walking Backwards," you do not lose ground but discover the stepping-stones of your own history.

- History is just facts until it is brought to life by people. The everyday lives of our ancestors can be living history for us.

- Each of your ancestors has contributed to a piece of you. Discover the richness of each piece.

- You must know where you have been in order to know where you want to go.

SUGGESTED READING

Memoirs and Family Writing

Hofmann, William J. *Life Writing: A Guide to Family Journals and Personal Memoirs.* New York: St. Martin's Press, 1982.

Knott, Leonard L. *Writing for the Joy of It.* Cincinnati: Writer's Digest Books, 1983.

Stillman, Peter R. *Families Writing.* Cincinnati: Writer's Digest Books, 1989.

Current and Historical Events

Daniel, Clifton, ed. *Chronicles of the 20th Century.* Mount Kisco, N.Y.: Chronicle Publications, 1987. Annual Chronicle of the Year updates.

Grun, Bernard. *The Timetables of History: A Horizontal Linkage of People and Events.* Rev. ed. New York: Simon & Schuster, 1982.

Trager, James, ed. *The People's Chronology: A Year-by-Year Record of Human Events from Prehistory to the Present.* New York: Holt, Rinehart & Winston, 1979.

The Journal as Time Machine to the Future

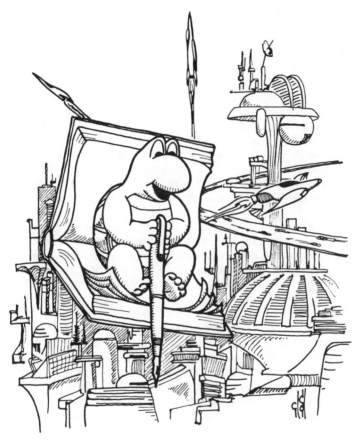

I dipt into the future far as human eye could see,
Saw the vision of the world and all the wonder that
would be.

—Alfred, Lord Tennyson
Locksley Hall

INTRODUCTION

What do you think your life will be like five years from now? Ten years? Fifteen? Twenty-five? Fifty?

With the movies *Star Wars, Robocop, Star Trek,* and *Back to the Future* so popular, we can certainly say "the future" is *in.* We may think about the future a lot, but that future is a world of the imagination, not reality. We may take space ships to Mars and operate our homes solely through automation, but we do these things imagining ourselves as no older than we are now. We don't like to imagine a future where we will be so old that we will *have* to operate everything automatically from our rockers. Since in our journals we will go there in our imaginations, we can certainly choose to imagine that medical science has advanced so much that we will have eternal youth.

What purpose, besides fun, can journaling to the future have? In journal writing we become aware of the mystery of time. We have traveled to the past, learning where we came from. We can now travel to the future to see where we are going. We can prepare for going there with more knowledge and poise, and with some excitement and healthy anticipation. We can see the balance of our lives, see our lives as a whole. We are born, we enjoy our unknown allotment of years, and we die. We see and accept this natural cycle for ourselves and those around us.

We can never know exactly what is coming for us around the corner, of course. We would never want to. Life would lose its sense of mystery, and we would lose our eager anticipation. Ursula LeGuin, in the wisdom she has gained from writing fiction about the future, has said that the only thing that makes life possible is the permanent, intolerable uncertainty, not knowing what comes next. But we can wonder and daydream and imagine. As long as we are fantasizing, we can also enjoy what might seem impossible.

A student said she didn't want to think about the future. She didn't want to imagine anything happening, because then it might happen. Don't we, for the most part, choose our own roads, create our own futures? If you have taken charge of your life, you are making your own choices and creating your own future. One of the things you may discover through journaling is whether you are a person who *lets* things happen or a person who *makes* things happen. Journaling can help you take charge and write your own life book.

PURPOSES AND AIMS

- To think about your future

- To speculate on what it might be like and to enjoy the possibilities

- To accept the passing of time as natural and to plan for it

- To learn to set goals

- To program success

A TITLE FOR YOUR LIFE

Let's start by giving your life so far a title. Think back over what has already happened and choose a title that seems to fit. It might be *The Crazy Adventures of Suzy Smith*, or if you have a big family, *One Life in the Smith Zoo*. If you are an only child, you might choose *Alone and Loving It*. If you have moved a lot, *Around the World in Three Thousand Days* is a possibility. *The Voice of Johnny Brown* or *Only One Me* might be appropriate. Be creative.

Now divide your life so far into chapters. Limit the number. Let's say your book is going to have twenty chapters. "I Was Born" will probably be chapter 1. You have lived ten and there are ten to go. The future chapters will probably cover larger chunks of time.

Your chapter titles might look like this:

1. I Was Born
2. I Got a Baby Sister
3. I Started to School
4. We Moved to Omaha
5. Second Grade
6. Third Grade
7. I Got My Dog
8. We Moved to California
9. Fourth Grade
10. Fifth Grade

But it is the next ten chapters we are more interested in writing about now. Imagine what they might be.

11. High School Football Star
12. My College Years
13. I Become a Stuntperson for the Movies
14. Eighteen Broken Bones
15. I Study Medicine
16. I Get Married
17. I Discover Miracle Plastic Bones
18. Saving the President
19. First Female Surgeon on Mars
20. I Die and People Say ...

Take any of the last ten chapter titles of your own book and write the chapter, exercising your imagination to the limit. What will your life be like? What other people will be in the chapter? How will you feel?

REMEMBERING THE FUTURE

> "It's a queer sort of memory that only works backwards," the Queen remarked.
>
> — Lewis Carroll
> *Through the Looking Glass*

Write about the future as if you were remembering it.

It is (*date*). I am thirty years old. I am just finishing my career as a ballet star. I have danced at all the great theaters in Europe. I have heard the applause, seen the standing ovations, reveled in the glory of being the best. I have danced for the king and queen of England twice. They have asked me to settle in London and start a ballet school there. They would like their son to study under me. I feel I could dance forever, but I want to retire while I'm at the top. I will live in my apartment in the city, keep my condo in New York, but look for a cottage in the south of England for privacy. All my hard work paid off, and I have lived life to the fullest. I am very happy.

Write a portrait of yourself at eighty years old. Describe yourself in detail at this age. How do you look? What are you doing? What are your hobbies? What work do you do? Where do you live? Who are your friends? Do you have children? Grandchildren? Do you travel? Are you in good health? Dialogue with yourself at eighty.

Me: You're eighty? That's really old.

Me at 80: Not really. I'm enjoying it.

Me: What can you do at that age? Just sit in your rocker and watch TV?

80: Of course not. I do watch all the tennis matches, but I play every day, too.

Me: You're playing tennis!

80: Sure. Didn't I start playing when I was ten? I played on the high school and college varsity teams. Why should I stop?

Me: You just stand there and pretend to play, don't you?

80: I'll have you know I'm ranked in the eighty-year-old division in the United States. Number three. I win a lot of tournaments.

Me: Yeah, but who's playing in them? Old people. Right?

80:       You could say that, if you think eighty is old. I'm leaving for Australia next week. Playing in the Aussie Seniors Open.

Me: I suppose you'll stop off and go surfing while you're there?

80:       You know, you always were a smart alec. I think you're getting worse. Go chase a kangaroo or get lost on Mars. I'm keeping my doubles partner waiting.

YOUR DREAM HOUSE, FUTURE WORK, AND SUCCESS

Have you ever thought about where you'd like to live if you could live anyplace in the world and what your house would look like?

Plan your house in your journal. Cost is no problem. What style is it? Draw pictures of the outside. Make a plan for the inside. Draw pictures of the rooms. Which is your favorite room?

Write descriptions of the house and all its rooms; include details about colors and furnishings. What special things does your house have? Timesavers? Automatic, futuristic devices? Collections? Places for pets? Musical instruments?

Where is this house? Describe the view from your bedroom window. What do you see at different times of the year? Take a walk around the outside and describe what you see, hear, feel, smell.

What do you want to be when you grow up? Familiar question? It is fun to think about. Think of the talents you have. Think of your hobbies, what you like to do. What subjects are your best at school? What subjects would you like to be good at? Are you good at sports, music, art, writing?

Now, list ten careers you think you would enjoy. Maybe some of them don't seem possible to you, but list them if you'd like to do them. No fair saying, "I couldn't do that." Rank them, listing the one you like best first.

Discuss that career. What skills, talents would you need to be successful at it? What would you have to do to prepare for going into that career? Maybe you don't know all you'd have to do, but write down what you imagine you'd need. Don't forget to list the personality traits you'd need for the career.

Now, imagine yourself following that career and write about it. Imagine yourself being successful at it. What would your life be like? How would you feel about yourself? What would the people around you say about you? What would they think about your success?

Let's think for a moment about being successful at any career. Let's think about being successful at living your life. Brainstorm, using the word "success" in the center of a cluster (see page 56). Clustering, sometimes called webbing, is a method of brainstorming where one surrounds the key word with other words or phrases which come to mind. If success is living the life you want to live, what do you need to feel successful?

Write a thought piece about success. Share this with your friends. What do they think success is? Do parents and teachers have other ideas?

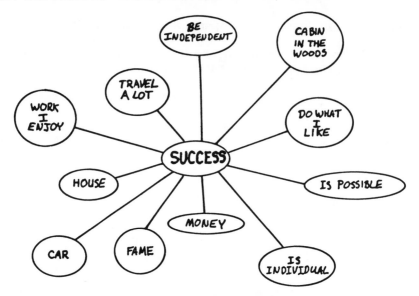

BACK TO THE FUTURE: PART TWO

Let's get a little crazy. We don't really know what is going to happen in our futures, do we? We are using our imaginations. Right? So we can make anything happen.

List your all-out wild and crazy fantasies. In your list use this format: "I am a _____." Think of all the things you'd like to do. Stretch things you can do now. Your list might look like this:

I am a rock star and I play guitar.

I am a country/western singer.

I am an undersea diver and explorer.

I am a space scientist and the first to land on and study Jupiter.

I am a famous concert pianist.

I am head of a company that manufactures futuristic toys.

I am a pro football star.

I am a space developer and have opened the first McDonalds on Mars and the moon.

I am leading the first expedition to the center of the earth.

I am a time traveler studying dinosaurs in the Mesozoic era. I have made pets of two species.

I am a well-known clothing designer.

I am a famous writer and poet.

Choose one or more of these fantasy careers to write about. What would your life be like? What would you do day by day? What would you wear? What is your salary? Write a news story with headlines about you. Pick an exciting moment in your life to tell about in detail. Maybe you won Super Bowl LVIII in the last thirty seconds, leading your team to victory. Tell us about your latest toy discovery, your undersea discovery. Tell us about your pet dinosaur, your latest book. Show us your style show for this season's clothing. This will be a part of your journal that will be fun to share.

YOUR OWN BUSINESS

Imagine that you are president of your own business. Think of what you'd like that business to be. Describe it in detail. How did you get started? What made you think of this particular business? Was it successful right away, or did you have to work hard to promote it? How did you promote it? What kind of advertising? Television? Mail? Telephone? Stunts? How many people do you have working for you? What do they do? What kind of money did you make in the beginning, then later when you were more successful? What ideas went wrong? What was your best idea that went right? Do you like working for yourself? Why, or why not? Interview yourself for an article in *Business Week* magazine. Will you ever get tired of this business? What will you do with it? Then what will you do next?

I own and run a restaurant just off the downtown Boulder Mall. It's called Barbara's Soup Kitchen. I have a limited menu, serving only one soup, chili, salad, pie, and bread, all homemade, of course. Here's the menu: (Remember there's chili every day.)

Monday: Vegetable soup; apple and blueberry pie

Tuesday: Potato soup; egg custard and coconut cream pie

Wednesday: Lentil soup with ham; peach and cherry pie

Thursday: Turkey and corn chowder; pecan and pumpkin pie

Friday: Chicken soup; chocolate and lemon meringue pie

Breads will include oatmeal, sesame wheat, garlic, and cornbread.

I'd close on Saturday and Sunday. I'd have a small dining room but there would be takeouts. I'd advertise some at first, but then have just a tiny ad and a listing in the Yellow Pages. Word of mouth would be the best advertising. There would be one price for soup and salad, pie, bread, coffee or tea: $6.50. I'd start out being open only at noon, but later I might add breakfast with my famous cinnamon rolls. I'd close at two and come home and write. I'd walk both ways to work so I wouldn't get too fat.

SETTING GOALS AND REACHING GOALS

Career people—in business, research, even politics and art—do not usually think about what they have done. They look and think ahead.

> *One never notices what has been done; one can only see what remains to be done.*
>
> —Marie Curie
> Letter to her brother, March 18, 1894

Artists, musicians, and writers are often asked what their favorite painting, concert, or book is. Most forget a work once it is finished. They think about what to do next. They get excited about a new work—what they will paint, compose, or write next. They enjoy the work at hand. What will you do next? What exciting ideas will you follow through on? What goals will you set?

List five things you'd like to accomplish in the next year. These may be new things. They may be extensions of things you are doing now. Here is a sample list:

- Raise my grade in math

- Learn a better tennis serve

- Improve my eating habits

- Make one new friend

- Read at least twenty new books

Or maybe you'd like to approach your list in a different or more creative way.

- Swim to California (keeping a mileage chart and map with pins to show my progress)

- Study Egyptian hieroglyphics

- Write a story or poem and see it published

- Design and sew my own Halloween costume, making it very futuristic

- Learn to speak Chinese

You can do anything you want to do. First you have to decide what it is that you really want to do. This is where many people fail. They can't decide what they *want* to do. Deciding is half the battle. Here are some ways to get what you want.

1. Decide what you want or want to do.

2. Find out how to go about it. This is like making a map or a guidebook.

3. Tell three people you are going to do it.

4. Write all this down in your journal. Remember the future. Write about it happening for you.

5. Break up your plan, map, or guidebook into small, small steps. Compare getting there to climbing a mountain. You can't just leap to the top. You have to take hundreds of tiny steps and keep going up. You may even slide back at times and have to start again.

6. Tell yourself every day that you can do this.

> *You must do the things you think you cannot do.*
> —Eleanor Roosevelt

7. Make a sign that announces your goal and post it where you will see it every morning and every night. Maybe it's a newspaper headline. (*Your name*) Becomes Famous Astronaut. (*Your name*) Has First Gold Disc.

8. Never give up, no matter how discouraged you may become.

9. Remember that there are no excuses for failure:

   Theodore Roosevelt was a sickly, asthmatic child. Sheer guts and determination made him a rancher, sportsman, war hero (he commanded the famed Rough Riders), and president of the United States.

   Franklin Delano Roosevelt was a victim of polio. He led the United States through two of our country's greatest crises, the Great Depression and World War II—from a wheelchair.

   Artist *Toulouse-Lautrec* could get around only on wheeled boards.

   Wilma Randolph couldn't walk at the age of seven. In 1962 she became a triple Olympic gold medalist in track and field.

   Tom Dempsey was born with half a right foot and two partial fingers on his right hand. He became a professional football player for the Philadelphia Eagles and in 1970 set a world record by kicking a sixty-three-yard field goal.

   Actress *Sandy Duncan* has only one usable eye but is a star of movies and television.

Ludwig van Beethoven wrote some of the world's greatest music even after losing his hearing.

Thomas Edison never finished grade school. What are some of his inventions?

Steven Spielberg's high school grades were so poor he couldn't get into film school. Have you seen any of his movies?

Sophia Loren's schoolmates called her "Toothpick." She was born poor, never had enough to eat, and was very much afraid of the dark because of so much time spent huddled in a crowded railway tunnel bomb shelter during World War II. She is now considered one of the world's most beautiful women.

Walt Disney's first company went bankrupt.

Grandma Moses didn't start painting until she was eighty.

CONCLUSION

The future belongs to you. Some planning will be like a road map, keeping you going on the path you choose. One of Laurence J. Peter's "principles" suggests that if you don't know where you're going, you may end up someplace else. Many people enjoy wandering through life. You have to know if you're one of those people. You have to know if you'll enjoy all the side trips you'll take if you have no plans. Even the best of planning will result in some unforeseen detours, but we recommend the journal as a place to take some of your trips in advance to see what might result.

> *"Will you tell me, please, which way I ought to go from here?" asked Alice.*
>
> *"That depends a good deal on where you want to get to," said the Cat.*
>
> —Lewis Carroll
> *Through the Looking Glass*

> *Hold fast to dreams, for if dreams die,*
> *Life is a broken-winged bird that cannot fly.*
> —Langston Hughes
> "Dreams"

❏ ❏ ❏

POINTS TO REMEMBER

- Traveling to the future can help you imagine where you are going.

- Imagining the future can help you see your life as a whole.

- Looking at the future should increase your anticipation, your excitement for living it.

- You are in charge of your life.

- The journal can help you program your successful future.

- Write about the future as if you were remembering it.

- What you thought of as a fantasy may be possible and desirable.

- Setting goals helps you reach a destination or get the things you desire and need.

- You can do anything you want to do. Tell your journal what you want to do with your life.

- The future belongs to you. Claim it in your journal.

CHAPTER
6

The Celebration Journal

I celebrate myself and sing myself, ...
— Walt Whitman
Song of Myself

63

INTRODUCTION

Many people tell us they write in their journals only when they are miserable. They use their journal self as solace, a friend in need. There is nothing wrong with that practice if it is balanced with recording happy moments and joyful times.

One of Dostoyevski's characters says, "Man is unhappy because he doesn't know he's happy. It's only that. That's all! If anyone finds out he'll become happy at once, that minute."

After devoting some time to this "happy practice," journal enthusiasts have discovered that "bad days" were often not as bad as they had perceived. By recording at the end of a bad day all the good things that happened, they find the day balanced or, more often, much more positive than they had thought. What they had done was focus on the one bad thing, letting it over-shadow dozens of small joys.

I am happy and content because I think I am.

—Lesage
Histoire de Gil Blas 1735

Writing down happy events has many positive spillovers into our lives. We develop skills of feeling deeply, of recognizing positive energy and using it. We find ourselves experiencing positive energy and using it. We find ourselves experiencing heightened sensory perception. We take joy in altering our world to make room for joy. We need no mind-expanding drugs, since we discover we already have the ability to experience life on a higher level than we had realized.

Psychologists have suggested that we learn more about ourselves by studying and learning *what makes us happy* than we do by focusing on worries and negative feelings.

Look for sorrow and you will see
Sorrow looking back at thee.
Look for joy and you will find
A steady companion, laughing and kind.

—Anonymous

PURPOSES AND AIMS

- To celebrate the joy in your life

- To learn to focus on happiness

- To look at our environment with appreciation and an awakened eye

YOUR FAVORITE THINGS AND SENSORY IMAGES

What are the small things that make you happy? Remember the song from *The Sound of Music* and make a list of *your* favorite things. Expand the items with sensory image. Instead of saying "a rose," say: "The first red rose of springtime beaded with diamonds of morning dew."

The black *M* on my cat's forehead

Rain on the attic roof when I wake

The smell of bread baking on a winter day

Peach-fuzz hair on a new baby's head

A saltwater breeze off the ocean

A junco hanging upside down on my bird feeder

Crickets fiddling on a summer night

Amber iced tea in a clear glass with a slice of yellow lemon

Soft, feathery snowflakes in a streetlight halo

The click of ice skate blades on a frozen lake

Call up a pleasant sensory image from as far back in your childhood as you can remember. Perhaps you remember snuggling in your mother's arms after you'd skinned your knee. The smell of hot cocoa when you'd come in from building a snowman. Walking barefoot in freshly cut grass, or on a beach. The scratchy stubble on your father's chin when you hugged him early in the morning. The smell of a new book or a freshly sharpened pencil the first day of school.

Describe the experience in detail, concentrating on the senses. Try to smell, taste, feel, see, hear what you are writing about.

If you carry your journal with you some of the time, and many people do, get in the habit of recording sensory images you experience as you travel through your day. This is a good thing to do while you're waiting for your appointment at the doctor or the orthodontist. We often have five or ten minutes of time to spare throughout the day. Use this time to capture small images you might forget by evening.

These small observations are a rich source for poetry or parts of stories you may write. Let's say you are writing a story set on the ocean, but now you are back home in Kansas. If you turn to the journal page where you recorded your sensory experiences while on vacation at the beach, you can drop those lines right into your story. The reader will say, "Yes, I feel as if I'm there. This author has been to the beach."

Gray-green waves with lacy foam edges, rush back and forth, chasing sandpipers. "Tag, you're it," the waves call, and the small brown and white birds turn, chasing back on tiptoe. Their feet leave a pattern of tiny *Y*s on the wet, packed sand. Quickly the ocean erases the footprints as it rushes back in, never tiring of the game.

I stand in the surf, laughing as the water pulls at my ankles. When it can't push me over coming in, it gobbles the sand out from under my feet going out. I lose my balance and fall, splashing salty water on my sister who squeals and runs.

Celebrate a simple thing such as a sunrise or a sunset.

As I paused just outside the closed door the eastern sky turned from rosy pink to burning red. And the clouds and the mountain peaks to the west, the entire sky, in fact, reflected that color, as if it came from some great unseen conflagration.... In spite of my weariness my heart lifted at the sight of the flaming sky. A silent celebration of Morning Prayers, I thought, a visual Matins and Lauds.

— Alix Ainsley
The House of Whispering Aspens

And now the evening redness deepens till all the west or northwest horizon is red; as if the sky were rubbed there with some rich Indian pigment, a permanent dye; as if the Artist of the world had mixed his red paints on the edge of the inverted saucer of the sky.... An exhilarating, cheering redness.

— Henry Thoreau
Journal, July 20, 1852

THINGS YOU DO WELL

Make a list of all the things you can do. Put a star by the ones you do best. These do not all have to be big things like playing the piano, ice skating, or painting. Perhaps you are the best leaf raker in your family. Maybe you are the best at dusting when your family cleans house. And furthermore, you *like* to dust.

Now think about dusting or playing the piano or baseball or swimming or running. Write a sensory image piece about something you like to do.

I waited in the on-deck circle, anticipating my turn at bat. Dirt around me had turned to soft, beige powder. Leaning the bat against my knee, I patted both hands on the flour-like surface of the ground. I rubbed it on my sweaty palms, leaving my hands dry and gritty.

"Batter up," the umpire yelled.

I took a deep breath of the moist spring air and walked to the batter's box. Giving home plate a satisfactory thud with the bat, I swished the air twice, hoping to intimidate the pitcher with the power of my swing. The bat had a solid feel, the hardwood resting firmly, yet relaxed, in my grip.

The first pitch zipped past my nose like a speeding bee. *Whoosh-thud*, it hit the catcher's mitt, sending an almost imperceptible cloud of dust into the air. Ball one.

I stepped back to still my pounding heart. Bases were loaded. If I could get a hit, we'd win the game. *Swish-swish*, I ripped the air again to relax. I patted my hard hat, stepped back in, crouched. The pitcher's grin blurred as I focused my mind and body for a hit.

Crack, the solid sound of a three-bagger split the silence as I connected. Grinning, I dropped my bat and dashed toward first.

HAPPY PRACTICE

List as many things as you can think of that make you happy.

Exciting things. What is the most exciting thing you've done in the past week, in the past month, in the past year. Write about it in detail. Why was it exciting? Remember all your feelings.

Happiest moments. List the happiest moments you can remember in your whole life. Choose one. Think of a metaphor for that moment: a roller coaster? a carousel with calliope blaring? a double chocolate fudge mocha almond ice cream sundae? a truckload of yellow roses? Write about it. Repeat this for any of the happy moments on your list.

Cut out a cartoon that reflects something in your life and paste it in your journal.

Draw an original cartoon of something funny or a happy event that occurred today.

Hard things. What is the hardest thing you've ever done? Write about it. Concentrate on your feelings.

Joy.   Write a list of today's joys. Dialogue with Joy.

Me: My, I'm glad to see you. Why don't you come more often?

Joy: I'm here all the time. You just have to recognize me. Look around you.

Me: I like the really big joys. My birthday and Christmas and summer vacation.

Joy: Then you miss a lot. Sometimes the little joys are more satisfying.

Me: Like what? What could be neater than my birthday?

Joy: Holding your cat in your lap and listening to her purr. Rubbing her velvet ears between two fingers gently. Having her lick your chin with her rough tongue.

Me: Sure, that's nice. I like it, but ...

Joy: That happens every day. Your birthday comes only once a year. I hope you aren't going to sit around waiting for 364 days to be happy again.

Me: Nah, I don't do that. I just never think about little things.

Joy: I challenge you to think about them. Enjoy them. You'll be surprised at how good you feel.

Me: You want me to become a Pollyanna?

Joy: No, I want you to be happy every day.

Me: Well, I guess it won't hurt to try it. If I don't tell anyone.

Joy: You can tell your journal.

Me: Okay, I'll try it for one week.

Favorite places. What is your
- favorite place of all?
- favorite place you've lived?
- favorite place you've traveled to?
- favorite place you'd like to visit?

Write about any of these. Be sure to include sensory images. Is there some kind of magic about this place? Write about the magic.

One favorite thing. What is your favorite thing in your whole house? Is there an inanimate object in your room or your house that you'd hate to have to live without—that if you moved, you'd take with you and when you'd put it in place, you'd say, Now I'm home again? People who have to travel a lot often take along something of this sort. We read of a man who always took a photograph of his family and set it on his dresser in a motel room, and of a woman who took a small patchwork quilt that was old and reminded her of home. She would spread it on her motel bed and make it her home away from home.

> *The need to define who you are by the place in which you live remains intact, even when that place is defined by a single object.*
>
> —Margaret Mead
> *Blackberry Winter*

Your favorite person. Who is your favorite person in the whole world? Write a portrait of this person. If your first answer was a family member, who is your favorite person outside your family? Don't forget to use color when you write a portrait. Perhaps your grandmother is a light shade of lavender and gray. Or maybe she's fire-engine red! Color often helps describe a person better than what he or she looks like or wears.

Your favorite pet. Write a portrait of your favorite pet—one you've had or one you'd like to have. Concentrate on sensory image in your description, details, and colors.

Colored pictures. Paint a picture of a piece of your life or something that happened to you. Use color to make it come alive. Don't forget to use shades, hues of the colors. You might choose one color or many colors.

> Today was one of the happiest days of my life. The whole day was shades of pink. Pink is my favorite color, so of course I'd think the day was pink. But it started with a sunrise that was all rose and mauve and salmon-colored. I could hardly believe my eyes when I got up and looked out the window. I knew right then it was going to be a great day. I wonder if sometimes because you think you're going to have a good day, you help make it good? I put on my new pink sweater and my gray skirt. I put pink barrettes in my hair. I laughed out loud when I found Mother had served cranberry juice for breakfast today. When I got to school and the drama teacher announced that I had the lead in the school play I about fainted. I had tried out and I had hoped, but I never dreamed I'd get it. I was sure that Rusty Rogers would win the part. She's such a good actress. I floated through the day on a pink cloud. Peter Woods said he had a hard time getting my attention, but I'm glad he did. He asked me to go to the spring fling. I'm sure I blushed, but of course I said yes.

> This morning when I took Missy for a walk the whole day seemed to have turned green. The lawn was an emerald carpet over the front yard. Tiny green daffodil blades pushed through the earth in the flower beds. Doilies of a darker green told me johnny-jump-ups would be the first to bloom. Tiny purple faces with yellow cheeks would soon peek through the lacy mat. Aspens had finished tasseling and now a pinch of green signaled leaves coming. Missy wanted to sniff everything. I think she could smell spring coming at last.

Time alone. Make a list of things you like to do when you're alone. Describe the joy of doing one of them, sharing only with yourself.

> *How sweet, how passing sweet, is solitude.*
> —William Cowper
> *Retirement*

CONCLUSION

Think of all this recording of your happy days as a savings account in your mood bank. You can dip into it when something doesn't go your way. Rereading about a time when you were happy will bring those good feelings back to enjoy over and over.

Keeping a journal is no guarantee that you will be happy, of course. But keeping a journal—recording everyday joys and joyous events—and practicing being happy are sure to have a positive effect on your life. Try it and see what happens.

POINTS TO REMEMBER

- Use the journal to celebrate yourself.

- The journal is a place to practice happiness and celebrate your joys.

- You learn more about yourself by observing what makes you happy than you do by focusing on negative feelings.

- The journal can help you learn to look at your environment with new eyes and appreciate what you see there.

- Your observations of your environment can be a rich source for poetry or stories.

- You do many things well. Use the journal to discover what they are.

- Recording your joys gives you a savings account to draw on when you need a lift.

The Journal as Self-Inspection and Reflection

As I walk'd by myself, I talk'd to myself,
And myself replied to me;
And the questions myself then put to myself,
With their answers, I give to thee.

—Bernard Barton
"Colloquy with Myself"

INTRODUCTION

Journal keeping can be an important tool for personal growth. It is a place to express feelings and thoughts, but equally important, it is a place to consider and examine those expressed feelings and thoughts. By looking upon ourselves as Main Characters we are more inclined to see ourselves as whole people who have excellent traits as well as faulty ones. We can discover abilities we've not credited ourselves with, and we can learn to examine our attitudes and find the reasons we hold them. To spend too much time in front of a mirror is neither healthy nor productive, but occasional study will help give us new perspectives and new outlooks.

PURPOSES AND AIMS

- To find and see ourselves as whole persons

- To get acquainted with ourselves

- To discover unnoticed abilities

- To look at and consider personal likes and dislikes

- To look at and consider personal attitudes, ideas, and feelings

- To carefully consider changes

REFLECTIONS

One of our first journal experiences was answering the question "Who am I?" (chapter 3). Now we want to learn more about "Who am I?" and also about "What I think, feel, believe."

The dictionary gives more than one definition for the word *reflection*: (1) giving back a likeness, showing an image, as in a mirror; (2) thinking about, giving careful consideration.

The writing exercises suggested in this chapter will act as a mirror whose reflections will help with self-inspection.

By looking in a mirror, you can tell how your hair is behaving, if you have jam on your face, and if your jeans are too short or too long. Your journal, too, can be a mirror — not to find out how you look, but, rather, to find out who you are. Your journal reflects your attitudes and moods, what you think and what you feel.

THE MAIN CHARACTER IS YOU

The main character in journal keeping is *you*. When writers begin to think about characters for their stories, they often use a character chart. These charts can be short, with just a few questions to answer, or they can be pages long with spaces for providing all kinds of detailed information. The purpose of a chart, long or short, is to learn about the character's personality, attitudes, and interests; background and environment; and physical appearance and abilities.

With you as the character, fill in this short character chart:

- Is your character a boy, a girl, a man, or a woman?

- How old is he/she?

- What is your character's name?

- What does your character look like? Height? Weight? Color of hair and eyes?

- What are your character's important physical abilities/disabilities?

- What kind of disposition does he/she have?

- What is your character's predominate personality trait?

- Does he/she have a family? Father? Mother? Brothers? Sisters?

- Are brothers, sisters younger or older than the character?

- What kind of friends does he/she have?

- Where does he/she live? Go to school? What grade?

- Does your character have any hobbies, jobs, after-school activities?

Now find some details that will help you to know more about this character—you. Complete as much of the list on page 76 as you can. Add more subjects if you wish.

My favorite kind of	My least favorite kind of
people_____	_____
animals	
pets_____	_____
other_____	_____
school subject_____	_____
hobby_____	_____
job_____	_____
sports	
as spectator_____	_____
as participant_____	_____
clothing_____	_____
food_____	_____
books_____	_____
music_____	_____
movies_____	_____
television shows_____	_____

PERSONALITY, ATTITUDES, AND INTERESTS

Likes and dislikes. Look over your lists of likes and dislikes. If you had made these lists last year would they have been different? A little different? Very different? Is there anything on one list that in the past would have been on the other list?

Choose one subject from your lists and think about why you feel the way you do.

> I hate snakes. And that's funny because I've never seen very many, just at the zoo. And no snake ever gave *me* any trouble. I think they mind their own business and so I guess it is the idea of snakes that I hate. I guess I'm not being fair to snakes to say I hate them. If I'm fair to them will they be fair to me? I am not going to try to find out.

Making pictures. Earlier in your journal writing you may have used a patchwork quilt as a metaphor. Now try making a collage, a picture using specific things that you remember. Your list of favorites and least favorites can help you. When you have arranged these remembered items into a mental picture, write about them. Discover why they are important enough for you to remember them.

My collage is made of things I remember from kindergarten. My picture has a house, flowers, a blue sky. It is mostly nice. After school I stayed with my grandmother. Her kitchen had wallpaper with little houses on it, houses with shutters and red brick chimneys. I used to pretend I really lived in one of those houses. So I have one in my picture. The flowers in front of the house are the gold stars Miss Kenyon put on my papers. The flowers are nice but the yard is ugly. It is the ugly brown and green plaid dress the girl who sat next to me wore almost every day. I hated her. She took my pencils and when I got them back they had teeth marks all over them. The blue sky is a robe my mother used to wear and those gray clouds are from a pair of corduroy pants I had to wear when everybody else was wearing jeans. So I guess that's why I like to see girls wear blue and feel like being rude to anyone wearing green and brown and wouldn't be caught dead wearing corduroy pants. I still feel happy when I think about Miss Kenyon and her gold stars.

More metaphors. You have already made metaphors about yourself. Now try some new ways of finding personal metaphor descriptions.
What would you be if you were a

bird	tree	color
animal	article of clothing	gemstone
flower	car	season of the year
vegetable	musical instrument	time of day

After you have written several comparisons, choose one to write about in more detail. Do you see yourself the same way you did when you first made up personal metaphors?

I think maybe once upon a time I was a cat because I like cats best and sometimes my eyes look like cat eyes. I am practicing learning how to purr.

I used to think I was like a brown moth but ever since Somebody told me I had nice eyes and hair I've felt more like a butterfly. If it hadn't been for that I'd still be a brown moth.

Special interests. Do you have a hobby or job? A favorite school subject, type of book, music, or television program? When did you get interested in this? Why do you like it? Has your interest encouraged you to try some other new activity? Think about the subject you choose to write about and see what discoveries you can find about your special interests.

BACKGROUND AND ENVIRONMENT

Now that you have done some inspection and reflection about how you see yourself and about your likes and dislikes, try exploring to find out how your background and environment might be influencing your feelings. Background and environment include family, friends, home, and school or job.

Attitudes. Do your family and friends share any of your attitudes about the items on your lists? Do their attitudes help to form your attitudes? Do you ever influence the way your friends and family think and feel?

Does where you live or where you have lived at some other time have anything to do with your choices? (Where you live includes the country you live in; city, suburb, small city, village, rural place; house, apartment, mobile home, etc.)

Do your school subjects, activities, teachers, classmates, and people you work with, affect your attitudes?

Choose from your lists one pair of likes and dislikes and look for the influence of others on your attitudes.

> Dad grew up on a farm and he could ride a horse as soon as he could walk (anyway that's what he says) so I've always wanted to have a horse. But this place won't even allow cats or dogs. So I guess because of my dad my favorite animal would be a horse if I could have one and my least favorite animal is a goldfish which is what the apartment house manager said I should get.

> My favorite people at school are the cheerleaders because now I'm a cheerleader. And my least favorite people *right now* are the girls who wanted to be cheerleaders and weren't chosen. I guess they're my least favorite people (*right now*) because I don't know what to say to them and I'm afraid that because I don't want to talk to them they'll think I'm stuck up.

> I don't like living in this town and I don't like going to this school and I don't like living in that dinky little apartment and if I could just go back home again and go to my old school and have my old friends I'd be happy ... I think.

Ifs. If you lived in another country or another culture, what do you think your life would be like? How might your present attitudes affect your living there?

If you lived at another time, future or past, what do you think your life would be like? How might your present attitudes affect your living then?

Study your lists of favorite and least favorite things and, from time to time, choose another one or pair to examine. How has your background influenced or not influenced your feelings and attitudes?

PHYSICAL DESCRIPTION AND ABILITIES

In your character chart you have already filled in some information about physical details. How would you describe your overall appearance? What do you think other people's first impression of you might be?

> I guess I am completely average. According to the charts, my height is average for my age and my weight is average. My hair is average brown and my eyes are average blue. Even my face is average— nothing too big or too little. I am so average I disappear when there are more than two people around.

Do you have special physical abilities or limitations? Outstanding physical ability might mean starring in sports, but it can also mean having an accurate eye, a keen ear, a steady hand.

Think about something you like to do that requires some sort of physical action or control. Write about how you do it, why you like doing it, and why it is important to you.

Think of some physical activity you don't do well and would like to do better. Write about your experiences and feelings.

List some special memories about your body that you can recall. What is your earliest body memory? Write something about it.

> First memory: Climbing out of my crib and being stuck back in. Other memories: Climbing onto kitchen counter to get cookies out of cupboard. Put back on floor with a smack on my seat.
> Climbing up the slide itself instead of the ladder. Getting yelled at.
> Climbing the tallest tree on our street.
> Mother yelling at me to get down out of there *right now* and if I fell she'd spank me good.

Write a dialogue with your body or a part of your body.

> Me: For Pete sake stop sneezing.
>
> Nose: I can't. *You* went out and caught the cold and *I'm* the one who suffers.
>
> Me: You're making everyone suffer listening to that ha choo Ha Choo HA CHOO! all the time.
>
> Nose: Do you think I'm enjoying it? Drip Drip, Rub Rub, Sneeze Sneeze. I HURT!
>
> Me: I'm sorry. I don't feel so great either. I guess I shouldn't take it out on you. Here, have another tissue.

OTHER REFLECTIONS

Do you have any superstitions? Where did they come from? How do you feel about them?

Choose a page at random from the dictionary. Use as many of the words as you can to talk about yourself.

Write descriptions or metaphors for your feelings about colors. What colors mean *happy, angry, lonely, excited, scared, peaceful*, and so on, to you?

> Lots of people say red is *angry*. Like He was so mad he saw red, Waving a red flag in front of a bull. I think red is exciting, happy. Red bows on Christmas packages, a red plaid shirt, the red of special sunrises and sunsets.

> Blue is cheerful, lavender is thoughtful, purple is — too much, pink is icky, and red is like KA-BOOM!

> Blue is dismal, lavender is sad, purple is kings and queens, pink is a lady, and red is *trouble*.

Make some lists about yourself using interests, traits, and habits that other people may not know about but that you feel can help describe you.

I am the sort of person who

- says hello to dogs
- reads the last page of a book first
- likes dill pickle and peanut butter sandwiches
- wants to learn to play the bagpipes
- thinks sleeping is a waste of time

MAKING CHANGES

As you look at and study your various reflections, do you find changes you'd like to make in yourself? Usually, changes in appearance, personality, talent, or ability are not nearly as necessary as changes in attitude. It is difficult for us to look at ourselves accurately and honestly, but neither can we be sure that the way we *think* other people see us is accurate or true. If we try to be everything we believe others want us to be, we'll end up satisfying no one. Do you remember Aesop's story of the man, the boy, and the donkey?

A man and his son took their donkey to market, but they found that they could not please anyone along the way. As they walked beside their donkey, they heard fellow travelers exclaim, "Such fools! Walking when they could be riding!" When the son rode the donkey there were shouts, "Look at that lazy boy — riding while his old father walks." When father and son changed places, the exclamations were, "Look at that lazy man — riding while his little son walks." But when they both got on the donkey, then the cries were, "Oh, shame! Overburdening that poor animal so cruelly!" Not knowing what else to do, the man and boy tried to carry the donkey between them. Not liking that, the donkey kicked them, and, as they crossed a bridge, its struggles knocked them all into the river.

Aesop's moral to the story is
PLEASE ALL AND YOU WILL PLEASE NONE

In the first century A.D., almost five hundred years after Aesop lived, a Roman philosopher by the name of Seneca gave similar advice:

What you think of yourself is much more important
than what others think of you.

Do you sometimes feel that others see you in a negative way? Are you sure the problem is the way others see you — or does the problem lie in the way you see yourself? Eleanor Roosevelt is quoted as having made a statement that should be copied into journals, posted on bulletin boards, and memorized:

Nobody can do anything to me that I'm not already
doing to myself.

Are there things about you that you feel you need to change? Do you think you need to make those changes because of put-downs you receive? Everyone receives put-down messages from other people now and then, but are some of these negative messages actually coming from *you*? Do you have a tape of self-put-downs that you turn on without realizing what you're doing?

You're stupid

What a klutz!

You're always making dumb remarks

You never do anything right

Why are you always making such an idiot of yourself?

Other people get along all right, why can't you?

You're hopeless!

Isn't it time to do a little tape erasing? Start by listing some of those self-put-downs and then record over them some positive statements about yourself.

I'm dumb.

I'm stupid.

I'm dumb in everything I do.

I got an F on my math test.

I'm dumb in math.

Am I dumb in *everything* I do?

I'm NOT dumb in everything I do!

I'll think of *something* I'm not dumb in.

I'm dumb in math but smart in history.

I get F's in math and A's in history.

I don't always get F's in math.

Sometimes I get C's in math.

I'm not as smart in math as I am in history.

I may not be as smart in math as I am in history, but
    I'm smart enough to pass math.

I'm not dumb in everything.

I'M NOT DUMB IN EVERYTHING!

I'm even smart in some things.

So there.

I'm so stupid in dance class.

I can't get that new step into my head — or my feet.

I'm a klutz.

I'm a klutz in dance class.

I'm a klutz in dance class but I'm not a klutz everywhere.

I'm not a klutz in swimming.

I'm a klutz in dance class but I won a blue ribbon in the
swim meet.

I'm not always going to be stupid in dance class — I just
haven't been at it as long as I've been swimming.

If I can win blue ribbons in swimming I can at least
learn a few dance steps.

It's not as if I wanted to be a dancer *all* my life.

I'll learn a few dance steps and I'll go on winning blue
ribbons in swimming.

I might even earn blue ribbons in something else.

In chapter 6, "The Celebration Journal," we talked about making lists of the things you do well. Go back now and look at those lists. Add some new things you've thought of, and continue adding things you do well. When you're tempted to start a new self-put-down tape, replay your THINGS I'M GOOD AT tape. Keep in mind that each of us has different talents and abilities.

The Mountain and the Squirrel
(A Fable)

The mountain and the squirrel
Had a quarrel,
And the former called the latter "little prig";
Bun replied,
"You are doubtless very big;
But all sorts of things and weather
Must be taken in together,
To make up a year
And a sphere.
And I think it no disgrace
To occupy my place.
If I'm not so large as you,
You are not so small as I,
And not half so spry.
I'll not deny you make
A very pretty squirrel track;
Talents differ; all is well and wisely put;
If I cannot carry forests on my back,
Neither can you crack a nut."

—Ralph Waldo Emerson

We can't all carry forests on our backs. Perhaps some of us aren't even very good at cracking nuts or at making squirrel tracks. But each of us can find things that we do—or can learn to do—well. J. G. Holland, a writer of the nineteenth century, said, "Every man who can be a first-rate something ... has no right to be a fifth-rate something; for a fifth-rate something is no better than a first-rate nothing."

The talent of success is nothing more than doing what you can do well; and doing well whatever you do, without a thought of fame.

—Henry Wadsworth Longfellow
Hyperion

BOOK TITLES AGAIN

In chapter 5, "The Journal as Time Machine to the Future," you thought about titles for your life. After all of these reflections and self-inspections, think of some more titles for the book in which the main character is *you*. Which title best describes you and your life right now? What title would describe the you of a year ago from your present perspective? What title best describes the way you would like your life to be, beginning tomorrow?

CONCLUSION

We have at various times referred to the journal as a friend who is always ready to listen. But we, in turn, can listen to the journal. The journal gives answers when we reread what we have written and see our ideas, attitudes, and feelings from the new perspective of reflection. The journal is a friend who listens to us, but to get acquainted with ourselves in positive, constructive ways, we need at times to stop and listen to what our journals are telling us.

POINTS TO REMEMBER

- Journal keeping is an important tool for personal growth.

- You are the main character in your life.

- The main character in your personal story grows and changes all the time through experience. The journal is a place to record and explore these changes.

- You are like a jigsaw puzzle with many pieces. A journal can help you see the whole picture.

- A journal can help you discover abilities you may not have noticed that you have.

- A journal can help you listen to the knowledge of your body.

- On occasion, stop and listen to what your journal is telling you.

SUGGESTED READING

Many books, fiction and nonfiction, can help with and provide insight into self-inspection and reflection. The following list is just a sample of the many books that touch on the ideas and topics discussed in this chapter.

Nonfiction

Kaye, Cathryn Berger. *Word Works*. Boston: Little, Brown, 1985. A book about writing, directed to young people. Chapter 8, "Keeping Track of Me," is devoted to journals, diaries, and logs.

Stein, Mark L. *Good and Bad Feelings*. New York: William Morrow, 1976. Writing for young people, a clinical psychologist explains and discusses five important good and bad feelings: anger, love, fear, happiness, and sadness.

Fiction

Bond, Nancy. *Another Shore*. New York: McElderry/Macmillan, 1988. Seventeen-year-old Lyn, working in a reconstructed colonial settlement in Nova Scotia, suddenly finds herself transported back to 1744.

Greenwald, Sheila. *Give Us a Great Big Smile, Rosy Cole*. Boston: Atlantic-Little, 1981. The humorous story of a ten-year-old facing up to comparisons with her older sisters and finding and accepting her own capabilities.

Lee, Mildred. *The Skating Rink*. New York: Seabury Press, 1969. Fifteen-year-old Tuck, uncertain of himself and mistrustful of those around him, justifies the confidence one person shows in him, and, despite physical and home-life handicaps, achieves changes and accomplishments for himself.

Lord, Betty Bao. *In the Year of the Boar and Jackie Robinson*. New York: Harper & Row, 1984. Bandit Wong, newly arrived from China, changes her name to Shirley Temple Wong and learns to roller skate and chew bubble gum as she strives to fit into a New York City fifth grade class.

O'Neill, Mary. *Hailstones and Halibut Bones*. New York: Doubleday, 1989. Poetry and metaphor about color.

Petersen, P. J. *Good-bye to Good Ol' Charlie*. New York: Delacorte, 1987. A family move to a new town gives Charlie the chance to find a new image—if he can just decide on one that fits him.

Peyton, K. M. *A Pattern of Roses*. New York: Crowell, 1973. A young adult novel with a touch of fantasy. Tim, with the help of Tom, a boy who lived at the beginning of the twentieth century, faces and makes decisions about his own talent and future.

CHAPTER 8

Using the Journal for Solving Problems and Making Decisions

What of me when my judgment wars with itself?
— Horace
Epistles

If you wish to know yourself observe how others act. If you wish to understand others look into your own heart.

— Johann Friedrich von Schiller
Votive Tablets

INTRODUCTION

Sometimes writing things out helps us find new ideas or new ways of approaching a problem that just thinking about or even talking about the subject can't do. Tristine Rainer in *The New Diary** points out that the diary is not a substitute for good friendship, but often in the process of writing our feelings about a question or a problem, we discover an inner wisdom that we've not credited ourselves as having. She also believes that problems, when confronted in journal writing, can change their negative energy into constructive energy. Each problem worked through helps develop our ability to meet the next challenge that arises. Recording a problem as honestly and accurately as we can, examining it by asking questions, experimenting with it by using dialogues, clustering, unsent letters, or other methods are all steps in clarifying and sorting out the many aspects of questions, decisions, or problems that we need to settle.

PURPOSES AND AIMS

- To look at the way we habitually make decisions and solve problems

- To find more effective ways of facing problems

- To learn to ask ourselves the right questions about a problem

- To experiment with different ways of searching for answers

- To understand that one of the hardest parts of solving a problem or making a decision is learning to face the issue with courage

FACING A PROBLEM

Think about how you usually solve problems or make decisions. Choose a metaphor to describe your way. Discuss it.

> Sometimes when I'm trying to solve a problem I feel as if I'm carrying a load of big rocks. I keep dropping them and picking them up and dropping some more, and I never get any place.

> Some people say they weigh a problem or a decision as if they could put the problem on a pair of scales. Whichever side of the problem has the most points going for it is the heaviest and it wins.

> Solving a problem is like putting a puzzle together. It's just a jumble of pieces until you get them in the right order. Then it all goes together the way it should.

---

*Rainer, Tristine. *The New Diary*. Los Angeles: J. P. Tarcher, 1978. P. 115.

All people have problems, but they do not handle them in the same way. Some people avoid thinking about a problem or pretend that it doesn't exist.

> Today was such a rotten day I almost quit school. Old Lady Jensen yelled so much I couldn't even think during the math quiz. I missed every basket in our PE tourney and came home and kicked the cat.

Some people identify their problems but do nothing constructive about them.

> She's not a fair grader. Next term I'll have a different teacher—I just need a little more time—I know, I know—I'll think about it tomorrow.

And some people

1. Identify the problem:

    - failing grade in math

2. Look for ways to do something about it:

    - study harder
    - spend less time watching TV
    - spend more time studying
    - ask for some help

3. Choose a plan of action:

    Starting tonight, I'll cut down on the TV and spend more time on math—time enough to *try* to understand it instead of just looking at it and giving up. And if this doesn't help, then in *one week* I'll ask *MS*. Jensen if she or somebody can give me help. *And if this doesn't work*—well, we'll see....

4. Follow through on the plan.

STEPS IN SOLVING A PROBLEM

Recording events, thoughts, and feelings will help you to recognize and identify problems.

Asking the right questions, making lists, and clustering are some of the ways to *examine* the problem and look for solutions.

Experimenting with letters not sent, dialogues, and writing from a different point of view are more ways to find solutions.

Some writers can plunge right into a discussion of their problems. Some approach the situation slowly by first writing about other activities, thoughts, and feelings of that day. And some may not be identifying the real problem at all. Perhaps the boy who missed all the baskets in the PE tourney thinks that his problem is his failure to score in a basketball game. By rereading journal entries, he can discover that his problems in PE actually start the period before—in Ms. Jensen's math class.

Asking the right questions. At times, the examining process will follow naturally after recording the problem. At other times, the writer will have to ask questions, not only to examine the problem, but, perhaps, even to discover the real problem.

The first and most important question to ask is:

What *do* I want?

not

What don't I want?

not — just yet —

How do I get rid of this problem?

but

What do I really want in this situation?

Scoring better in basketball?

Treating the cat more kindly?

Passing math?

Getting along better with everyone at school?

I'm not sure just what my problem is. Do I just want to get people off my back about book reports? Or do I want to try some other way of letting people (including Miss T.) know about some good books I think they'd like? Or do I just want to draw pictures instead of writing all the time?

When you identify the problem situation and decide what situation you would like in its place (What *do* I want?), then you can start exploring with what, why, and how questions.

Problem: Not getting my book reports in on time

How does this make me feel? Guilty, but then when everybody starts yelling at me, I feel mad.

Why do I feel this way? Guilty because I know I should be getting my reports in, and mad because no one likes to get yelled at.

What would I like changed about this? Not to have to write book reports.

Why? Because I never can make what I think about a book fit the way Miss T. wants the reports written.

How could this be changed? Miss T. could let us do some of our reports in different ways — draw pictures, talk about the book, write reports any way we want.

What could I do about this? Talk to Miss T.

How would that help? Maybe she doesn't understand how hard it is to always fit a book into her outline.

How should I go about this? Very carefully. Talk to her when she and I are both in a good mood. (Not yelling, not being yelled at.) Maybe show her some samples of what I mean.

Other ways of exploring problems. Clustering would be another way to explore feelings about a problem, about reasons there is a problem, and about possible solutions.

Experimenting with other kinds of writing can help you learn to look at personal problems from new points of view.

Dialogue with Self

Me:	Okay, so I was top scorer for the Blues until two weeks ago, so what happened? If you know so much, just tell me what happened.
Other Me:	You're mad. All the time you're mad. Just listen to yourself.
Me:	Well, why shouldn't I be mad, everybody jumping on me about everything—
Other Me:	Everybody? Everything?
Me:	Well, Ms. Jensen, Coach, missed baskets, grades, stuff—
Other Me:	I thought you made an A in science and B's in English and German last term.
Me:	Yeah, I did.
Other Me:	So?
Me:	Okay, so it's math that I'm getting yelled at about. Every day. And by the time I get to PE I'm so mad— Oh.
Other Me:	Oh?
Me:	So it's math, not basketball, that's my problem—

List what you consider some of your immediate problems. Choose one and write about it. Have you ever written about this problem before? If you have, compare your entries. How are they similar? How are they different?

In writing about this problem:

- Have you examined your feelings?
- Have you examined reasons for or causes of the problem?
- Have you examined possible remedies or solutions?

Ask yourself what, why, and how questions about this problem.

- Cluster reasons for the problem.
- Cluster feelings about the problem.
- Cluster solutions for the problem.

Dialogue and new point of view. Using a problem you have written about, create a dialogue between you and someone involved with the problem. Write what you would say and what you imagine that other person would say. After you have tried that, change places with that person. Discuss the problem from that person's point of view. Using the other person's point of view, write a dialogue about a problem between you and a teacher, parent, brother or sister, friend, or some other person.

Make a list of people who have helped shape your life, who have influenced you in some way. Are any of those on your list people you could go to to talk about a problem?

Choose someone from your list to dialogue with about a problem.

If you think two people on your list would have different ideas about your problem, dialogue with each of them, then write a dialogue between the two of them about your problem.

Dialogue between Me and My Friend Nan

Me: I've about decided to sign up to work on the school magazine.

Nan: You can't do that. You promised to be on our hockey team.

Me: I didn't promise, I said I might.

Nan: With you that's as good as a promise. Besides, you don't want to work with all those kids you don't even know.

Me: I'd get acquainted, and I like Miss Noel.

Nan: You think you'll get a better grade if you work on her magazine.

Me: No, I just think—

Nan: If you'll just *think*, you'll know you'd rather play hockey.

Dialogue between Me and Miss Noel

Me: I don't know. I sort of promised to be on the hockey team again.

Miss N: Promised?

Me: Well, I said I might.

Miss N: Would you rather play hockey than work on the magazine?

Me: I guess I know more about hockey. I feel awfully dumb, trying to help on the magazine when I don't know anything about it.

Miss N: You know, that's why we have school magazines and newspapers — so people can learn how they're written and published. We need to have new students learning all the time.

Me: Maybe somebody new instead of me should be playing hockey this term. What do you think?

Miss N: Oh no! It's not what I or anyone else thinks. It's entirely up to you. Deep down, honestly, what do *you* think?

Letters not sent. Write a letter to someone on your list about a problem you are having. Then write an answer as if from that person. Write a Dear Abby letter about a problem, then write Abby's answer.

DECISION MAKING

How do you make decisions? Is your method helpful? Does it leave things to chance? Does it consider reasons for and reasons against? Write about the way you usually make decisions.

Is there a decision now that you need to make? For example, you might want to go to camp this summer, but you also want to earn some money by working at the Ice Cream Shoppe.

Make a list of reasons for going to camp and a list of reasons against going to camp. Then make "for" and "against" lists about working at the Ice Cream Shoppe.

Write a letter to a friend who is working at the Ice Cream Shoppe about what you are doing at camp.

Write a letter to a friend at camp about your job at the Ice Cream Shoppe.

Write dialogues with a friend, parent, teacher, or some other person about your summer experiences.

Write a headline or an entire story for an interview by your school newspaper about your summer experience:

JOHNNY JONES SAYS CAMP EXPERIENCE
WORTH MORE THAN MONEY IN BANK

In considering the decision you need to make, have you asked yourself, "What do I want?"

What *do* you want?

- A summer of fun?

- A summer of earning your own money?

Does what you really want reach beyond the summer?

- The camp experience as preparation towards being a junior counselor?

- Money towards your own car, new guitar, dancing lessons?

As you think about what you want, don't limit yourself just to the things that seem possible. Do you want *both* camp and job? Write about it.

> No matter how many ways I try to decide *Which*, I keep coming out with *Both*. I wonder if anybody else has that kind of problem. I wonder if anyone else wants to go to camp or Disney World or Europe or Grandma's house and wants to work, too? HEY—That's an idea! If I could find that someone, maybe Mr. W. would let us split the Ice Cream Shoppe job, one of us the first six weeks, the other one the last six weeks. And I wouldn't have to stay at camp for both sessions and—

Dialogue with Mr. W. or write about your idea from his point of view. Cluster to come up with more ideas that don't seem possible.

After you've examined decision making in every way you can think of (clustering to find more ways), then think about a wider view of problem solving and decision making:

- Cluster around the word Change and then write about Change.

- Cluster around the word Risk and then write about Risk.

- Cluster around the word Possibilities and then write about Possibilities.

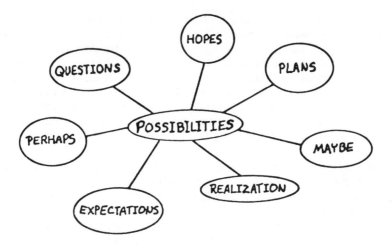

THE FINAL CRITERION

> *Criterion:*   a standard of judging, a rule or test by
> which something is tried or measured.

As you have worked on making decisions and searched for answers to problems, you have discovered that many times there are no *yes-no, right-wrong, this-not-that* answers. The factor in finding the final answer may well be your own feelings about the question.

Feelings of, "Well, I'm going to do it my way, I don't care what anyone else wants," aren't likely to lead to satisfactory solutions. Neither are feelings of, "Well, I'll just go along with what the others want." So how can you be sure your feelings about an issue are safe to follow? Again, it is a matter of asking the right questions.

1. Does the course you plan to follow seem sensible to you? If you have written about it, explored your feelings, asked what-why-how questions, dialogued, and clustered, you probably have already decided this is the sensible way to go.

2. What will be the effects of your action? Are you looking at it from the short view or the long view? How does it fit with your personal goals? Will what seems good right now seem not so good later on? How do all those bags of great-tasting taco chips this month measure up with complexion problems and extra pounds next month? In less personal and more outreaching problems, if you go ahead with your decision, will others benefit from it, or might they be hurt? And then, what would happen if everyone followed your decision? Would the results hurt or help others?

3. Is your course of action an honorable one? How will you feel about yourself when you have carried it out? How would certain individuals you respect, and by whom you want to be respected, feel about your action? Deep down, would you be hoping that they would never know?

> If I go with the guys I know I'll be breaking training but there's no way anyone would ever know except just us. All the guys say so. But Coach has spent so much extra time just helping me it doesn't seem quite fair to him — I think if he did know he'd be more hurt than mad. So even if he didn't know, how would I feel the next time I face him? But I'm so fed up with never going out and having some fun and being crazy and the guys keep telling me to come along. Breaking training once in a while doesn't seem so terrible does it? I don't know — I just don't know —

Would answering the criterion questions help this person? Have you had a decision that the questions could have helped with?

Marcus Aurelius, a Roman emperor who lived almost nineteen centuries ago, once wrote, "Never esteem anything as of advantage to thee that shall make thee break thy word or lose thy self-respect." Perhaps those words might be the real criterion in personal problem solving and decision making.

THE EXTRA ELEMENT

In looking at decision making and problem solving we have discussed methods for recognizing and identifying problems and ways of examining them and looking for solutions. Perhaps we have not said enough about how difficult it is to make some decisions; we certainly have not said anything about how difficult it is, once certain decisions are made, to carry them through.

After you have decided on the possibility of sharing the Ice Cream Shoppe summer job so you can also go to camp, you will probably be excited about carrying out the necessary details. But if you've decided to quit eating junk food you may find it hard to say no to the bag of taco chips. In some other situation you may find it painfully difficult to say you're not going to do it when pressured by friends or acquaintances. And you may find it almost impossible to turn off that self-put-down tape that whispers — or shouts — Ha! You'll never do it — you never follow through on anything.

These are the times you need the extra element, and that element is called *courage*. Courage is the ability to act effectively (capably, suitably, decisively) in the face of danger or difficulty. Courage is not the absence of fear. There is no such thing as courage if there is no fear. You can't be brave if you're not afraid.

It took courage for Saint George to pick up his lance and shield and go out to fight the dragon, but everyone has dragons, big and little, to fight. We don't always remember that we have lances and shields, too.

Your journal can be a most important lance and shield. Go back and reread how you faced other problems. Write through any fears you may be having about a decision, made or as yet unmade. Facing a fear directly will help you find the courage you need

- to say yes to yourself

- to say no to yourself

- to say no to others

- to express your opinions and feelings

- to stand firm for what you truly feel is right

- to stand firm for what you feel is right without hurting others

- to keep erasing those self-defeating tapes you've been storing and playing for so long

The Suggested Reading list at the end of this chapter includes a number of books in which individuals struggled and suffered but, in different ways, found the courage they needed, first to make and then to follow their decisions.

CONCLUSION

Problems seldom have easy answers. Learning to face them, explore them, look for new approaches to them, take the long view rather than the short view, and follow through with courage are big steps in growing and maturing and in understanding both self and others.

POINTS TO REMEMBER

- The journal is your number one assistant for solving problems.

- To find the right answer, you first have to find the right question.

    What is the problem?

    How do I look at problems?

    What do I want in the situation?

    Am I trying to do something constructive about what I want?

- When looking for the solution, try different ways of looking at the problem.

- The journal can help you rehearse future behavior in order to solve a problem.

- Decision making is a learned skill. The journal can help you improve and polish your skills.

- If there is no yes-no, right-wrong answer for a problem or decision, your feelings may be the deciding factor.

- Courage is the extra element in solving problems and making decisions.

SUGGESTED READING

Nonfiction

Aaseng, Nathan. *The Problem Solvers: People Who Turned Problems into Products*. Minneapolis: Lerner, 1989. For children.

Burns, Marilyn. *The Book of Think (Or How to Solve a Problem Twice Your Size)*. Boston: Little, Brown, 1976. For children.

Dorn, Lois. *Peace in the Family: A Workbook of Ideas and Action*. New York: Pantheon, 1987. See especially "Keeping a Journal." For adults.

Moorman, Thomas. *How to Work toward Agreement*. New York: Atheneum, 1979.

Fiction

Allan, Mabel Esther. *The View beyond My Father*. New York: Dodd, Mead, 1977. After Mary Anne suffers years of near-blindness and blindness, an operation restores her sight and gives her the chance to see and make decisions beyond her father's narrow and puritanical views. For older children.

Bulla, Clyde Robert. *The Chalk Box Kid*. New York: Random House, 1987. Nine-year-old Gregory's yard doesn't have room for a garden like his classmates' gardens, so he creates a surprising and different one in an unusual place.

Dygard, Thomas J. *Winning Kicker*. New York: William Morrow, 1978. Decisions have to be made by the town, the high school, the coach, the football players—and the girl—when a girl qualifies for a place on the football team.

George, Jean. *My Side of the Mountain*. New York: Dutton, 1959. During a year of living off the land in a home he has made for himself, thirteen-year-old Sam Gribley learns self-sufficiency.

Porte, Barbara Ann. *Harry's Dog*. New York: Greenwillow, 1984. An amusing, problem-solving story in which Harry and his aunt find a way for Harry to have a dog even though Harry's father is allergic to dogs. For younger children.

Riddell, Ruth. *Haunted Journey*. New York: Atheneum, 1988. When young Obie takes on the responsibility of saving his family's land, he faces many problems and decisions because of his mean-spirited family and the journey he must make through Tennessee wilderness, which is protected by ancient Indian spirits. For middle-grade children and older.

Sperry, Armstrong. *Call It Courage.* New York: Macmillan, 1971. This Newbery Award book tells about a South Seas boy, his fear of the sea, and the decision and courage it takes for him to face his fears. For middle-grade children.

Steiner, Barbara. *Oliver Dibbs and the Dinosaur Cause.* New York: Four Winds/Macmillan, 1986. Oliver is involved in a project to make the stegosaurus the state fossil while he works on his personal problems with the class bully. For middle-grade children.

Turkle, Brinton. *Do Not Open.* New York: Dutton, 1981. Using courage and imagination, Miss Moody vanquishes a dreadful creature that comes out of a bottle washed up from the sea. A picture book for all ages.

The Journal as Catharsis

*If you suffer, thank God! — it is a sure sign
that you are alive.*

—Elbert Hubbard
Epigrams

Joy comes, grief goes, we know not how.
— James Russell Lowell
The Vision of Sir Launfal

INTRODUCTION

The word *catharsis* is variously defined as a technique to relieve tension and anxiety; a cleansing or purifying; an emotional release. Journal writing can be a catharsis when it helps an explosion of emotion to escape, to free itself. The journal is the place for honest expression of feelings, whether those feelings reflect the reality of the situation or not. After the first outpouring, continued writing can often lead gradually to deeper, more thoughtful contemplation of the situation.

PURPOSES AND AIMS

- To learn to use the journal as willing confidant, sympathizer, and safety valve in times of emotional stress

- To understand that catharsis, the emotional release, can be an important part of experiencing high excitement such as anticipation, discovery, joy, and jubilation

- To understand that writing about personal grief, anger, or hurt not only helps to release pent-up emotions, but also helps to release the pain

- To learn to continue to write out feelings and thoughts after the first emotional entries, as a way of working through the pain and shock of anger, disappointment, or loss

WRITING AT THE HEIGHT OF EMOTION

The seventeenth-century English writer John Ray said, "A joy that's shared is a joy made double." But sometimes there is no person with whom to share a joy. The poet William Blake wrote, "I was angry with my friend;/I told my wrath, my wrath did end." But how did he tell his wrath and to whom? At times, personal confrontations are important, even necessary. But, often the journal is not only the safest and most helpful place to express intense emotion, it is also the most available and dependable place.

As with all journal writing, cathartic writing has very few shoulds or should nots, musts or must nots, other than:

- to write quickly
- to put down whatever comes to mind
- to write without judging, censoring, or editing
- to express personal feelings with honesty

Honesty here means stating real feelings. Those feelings may or may not be the truth of the matter.

THIS DAY HAS BEEN ABSOLUTELY-COMPLETELY-
AND-DEFINITELY, INDUBITABLY-UNEQUIVOCALLY-
AND-UTTERLY THE BEST DAY OF MY ENTIRE LIFE!

I HATE HER! I HATE EVERYBODY!!
EVERYBODY HATES ME!!!

Exaggerations of these kinds help with the immediate expression of intense feelings. In the case of distressing experiences, it speeds getting them out, distancing their corrosiveness, lessening their pain. Later, it will be easier to assess the situation and accompanying feelings objectively by reviewing written feelings than by reviewing broken dishes, kicked cats, or shouted words. An interval between writing and reading might even let us find some hints of humor in the event. An intense emotional experience may need writing about at different times before it is worked out, but eventually cathartic writing can lead into the exploring and examining that is necessary for help and healing.

Moments of elation can usually be shared, in part at least, with friends or family. Often, however, the fullest, deepest feelings are best shared only with one's journal. At times there are joyful, exciting events that cannot be shared with people. And even when they can be shared, discussed, and replayed with others, the journal sharing will be there to reread and relive over and over, long after friends have lost interest in the subject.

HIGH OCCASIONS

In chapter 6, "The Celebration Journal," you wrote about things that make you happy, that bring you joy. Shakespeare, in one of his sonnets, wrote, "Joy delights in joy ...," but there are times that others can't or won't delight or even want to share our own happiness and joy. Sometimes there is no one around to listen.

> When I got home from school today nobody else was home yet, but there was a very business-like looking letter addressed to me. It was from THE MAGAZINE! And when I opened the letter and read it I walked all around the house and read the letter in the kitchen and again in my room and again in the front hall. I started to call Suzy but then I remembered she had to go to the orthodontist's. I tried to call Gram three times but her line was always busy. I thought about calling Mom at work but decided I'd better not. I thought, until I read this letter to *somebody*, it won't really be true! I WON FIRST PRIZE IN THE NATIONAL POETRY CONTEST! Then, of course, I thought about my journal—Old Faithful! I could at least tell you about it.

There are times when it doesn't seem fair or kind to try to share a happy event.

Well — I made the first team — but Jeff didn't. Always before, we've done things together, talked them over together, shared the good and the bad and here I am so happy about making the team I'm about to explode. But I can't talk about it to Jeff — at least not yet. And I'm so disappointed and sorry that he didn't make it I could HOWL — but I made the team! I did!! I DID!

Often other people are too busy to listen or just don't understand what we want to tell them.

People sure are funny! And I don't mean funny-ha-ha. Peter Delancy O'Neil III is one week old today. He is absolutely beautiful and I want to hold him and talk to him and tell him I'm his big sister. I'd tell him I'm glad he's here and I'm glad I'm not an only child any more and that I'm not upset or jealous or any of those things Nana and Aunt Jen and Mama keep talking about when they think I'm not around. And when I try to tell them how much I like him they quickly suggest we go get some ice cream or play Monopoly or do *something entertaining* and if I couldn't at least write down how sweet and funny Peter is maybe I really would have a tantrum like they seem to think I'm going to any minute.

Looking forward to an exciting event, thinking about it ahead of time — *anticipation* — can be almost as exciting as the event itself. But some people don't understand that.

Today Janie said if I said one more word about starting riding lessons next month she'd sit with someone else at lunch and quit walking home from school with me. But it's all I can think about and so it's all I can talk about. So I guess I'll have to do my talking to someone else — well, okay Journal, here goes....

Things that give us pleasure, happiness, or joy are not always events to celebrate with fireworks and shouting. Sometimes we find unexpected moments of happiness that are too personal to share immediately with others, yet we feel we must express our feelings and acknowledge how important those moments are to us.

> *Not by appointment do we meet delight*
> *Or joy; they heed not our expectancy;*
> *But round some corner of the street of life*
> *They of a sudden greet us with a smile.*
>
> — Gerald Massey
> "The Bridegroom of Beauty"

Such moments, large or small, first recorded in a journal, might well go on to be the inspiration for a poem, a painting, or a song.

PAINFUL EXPERIENCES

Usually it is easier to tell others about our happy moments and our good times than it is to talk about the bad times. Even if we know we'll be discussing them, explaining them, or even asking for help with them at a later time, writing our feelings out first can help put our thoughts about them in some sort of order.

Anger. Name ten things that make you angry.

I get angry when _____

Look up some synonyms for the word *angry*.

Wrathful	enraged	irate
irritated	annoyed	vexed

There are many degrees of anger. Do all of the things on your list make you angry? Or do they annoy, irk, or merely bother you?

How do you express anger? How do you express annoyance? Think of metaphors to describe the way you show various degrees of anger.

> When I'm mad I'm like a thunderstorm. I bang and crash and knock things around.

> When I'm angry I turn into an icicle, freezing cold but sharp enough to hurt somebody. But then when somebody does something nice for me, I begin to melt.

Write a dialogue between you and the person, thing, or situation that makes you angry.

Me: You make me so mad! Annie, you just make me so mad—

Annie: What? I don't know what you're talking about.

Me: Yes you do. Well—anyway, you should.

Annie: I know you say you're mad. At me. Why?

Me: Because every time I tell you about something I've just gotten or something I've done, you just answer by telling me something you've got or done that's better. That's why! And it's not fair.

Annie: Nobody ever said life's fair and besides, I don't do that.

Me: Yes you do. You never listen to me.

Annie:	Sure I do. I heard you telling about a show you saw yesterday.
Me:	I was telling other people that.
Annie:	But I was listening too.
Me:	That's not the same. I mean when you and I talk.
Annie:	Well, maybe you need to talk more to other people.
Me:	Maybe you're right. Maybe I just should talk to other people. Talk to other people and listen to you.
Annie:	Hey — that's not fair —
Me:	Whoever said life's fair? Huh?

Dialoguing or writing from another point of view can give new perspective to the reasons for anger. Sometimes it uncovers an underlying cause for the anger, helping to answer the what, why, and how. And sometimes dialoguing or writing from another viewpoint can bring out bits of humor in the situation.

Even though the conversation is imaginary, often words expressed in the privacy of one's journal can do more good than an actual person-to-person dialogue. Angry spoken words will bring angry spoken answers, causing more anger, more misunderstandings, and more hurt feelings. Writing about anger gives time to work through it without interruption and without additional misunderstandings.

Envy and jealousy. Anger at times rises as a result of other emotions such as envy and jealousy.

> *envy:* feeling resentful, unhappy, spiteful because of desire to have an object or advantage possessed by someone else
>
> *jealousy:* feeling suspicious, intolerant, resentful about a rival

What makes you envious or jealous? Write about the last time you felt that way.

I am so mad at Deena I don't know if I'll ever speak to her again. She was with me when I discovered the sweatshirt at the Ecology Shop — black with white zebras marching around it. I loved it and wanted it, but I didn't have the money — Mrs. M. still owes me for the last two baby-sitting jobs and I'm mad at her too. Deena knew I wanted that shirt. I had my heart set on wearing it to Ally's birthday party but I couldn't get it right then because of the money. AND THEN — AT THE PARTY — DEENA'S PRESENT TO ALLY WAS THAT VERY SHIRT!! I am so mad I am a tornado.

I am a hurricane. I am angry like I've never been before. Anger at Deena, envy because Ally has my shirt. And jealousy. Because Ally not only has my shirt but obviously she has Deena's friendship that I thought — well, Deena isn't, can't be my best friend any more, and I'm so angry — *angry* — ANGRY — that ... I'm ... scared!

Dialogue with that little green creature inside you who finds things to envy and people to be jealous of. Find out what it has to say.

Fear. What are you afraid of? We can be afraid in a situation where we feel we are powerless to do anything. Sometimes we're afraid of the consequences if we *do* do something. And at other times we are simply afraid of the unknown.

Make a list of things you are afraid of.

1. I am afraid to cross the street at Park and Tenth. Twice now cars running red lights have just missed me.

2. I'm afraid to even think about, much less write down, how I feel about a certain person who shall remain nameless.

3. I'm afraid of starting the new school when we move and I don't know if it's because of that enormous building or the strange teachers or all those faceless kids.

Write about one of your fears, asking and answering some what-why-how questions. Then dialogue with that fear.

Failure. A fear that might be on your list is fear of failure. If this is one of your fears, ask yourself what-why-how questions about it.

- What are my feelings when I think I've failed?
- Why do I feel that way?
- Why do I think that I've failed?
- How do I deal with it when I really have failed?

Dialogue with that other little gremlin, the one who sits on your shoulder and tells you that you're not going to succeed.

Loneliness. Being lonely and being alone are not necessarily the same. To understand the difference, make some lists:

I am lonely when _____

When I'm alone I like to _____

Write about being alone:

I like to be alone sometimes because _____

    or

I never like to be alone because _____

Dialogue with your loneliness.

Create metaphors that describe your feelings of loneliness. What would loneliness be if it:

Were a color?

A musical instrument?

A song or a type of music?

A sound?

A place?

A time of day or time of year?

Now, using these same terms or others, make metaphors about the various aspects of being alone or of being lonely.

- Loneliness is gray fog, seeping in under doors and around windows.

- Quiet times are like harp music at twilight.

- Loneliness is everyone outside laughing and having fun when I'm inside working.

- Being alone can be like a cello playing "The Swan."

- Being lonely can be like exercises on an out-of-tune violin.

Misunderstandings and hurt feelings are often a part of loneliness.

People misunderstand me when _____

I feel hurt when _____

Write about what happened and how you felt when you were misunderstood or when your feelings were hurt. Make a regular journal entry or write an unsent letter to the person involved.

> Dear Deena,
>
> I *can't believe* you would do such a thing to someone you called a friend! You *knew* how I felt about that zebra shirt, but you bought it and you *gave it to Ally*! You could have found some other way to say that we aren't friends any more.
>
> Lou

After you have written out how you feel about a hurtful situation or misunderstanding, explore further the what-why-how of your feelings by writing from the other person's point of view. As you keep writing, don't be surprised if you find that your feelings are changing.

Dear Lou,

You're right. We're not friends any more.

Deena

Dear Lou,

I don't see why a little thing like a sweatshirt should keep us from being friends. Let's talk.

Deena

Dear Lou,

I knew you wanted that zebra shirt, but I thought you wanted it for a present for Ally. The next day the clerk in the store told me it was the only zebra shirt left. I tried three times to call you before Ally's party, but you never called me back. I thought you'd be glad Ally got the shirt.

Deena

Me: Likely story, Deena.

Deena: You mean you don't believe me?

Me: Would you believe a story like that?

Deena: Listen—we went into that store to get a present for Ally, remember?

Me: Yeah, I guess we did.

Deena: And I said, I'll bet she'd like this shirt.

Me: And I said I love it, I'm going to get it—only I didn't have the money then, so ... I see. I guess we were talking in two different directions.

Losses. A loss usually means grief—a large loss means a large grief, but small losses with their small griefs can hurt and be difficult to handle, too.

A loss that hurts could be someone's losing your book that was a birthday present from your grandfather. It could be, and often is, the loss of a good friend who must move away. Another kind of loss happens when someone who has been a friend chooses to spend his or her time with other people. Or the loss could be one brought about by death — the death of a family member, a friend, a much-admired public figure, a pet.

Talking out your hurt and sorrow with a good friend is one way to find help and healing. Sometimes, though, friends aren't around; sometimes even friends aren't willing to listen, or they just don't understand. But your journal is there, waiting. It always has time, it won't misunderstand, it won't be impatient. No loss is too big or too small for it to help you with.

Our reactions to loss are often confusing. We expect to be unhappy, but sadness and sorrow can be mixed up with feelings of guilt and anger. Denying the situation is part of grieving, too, and depression is the reaction that often lasts the longest. These periods don't necessarily come in a certain order or last for a certain length of time, but they need to be understood as a natural part of grieving and then worked through by talking or writing about them.

Feelings of guilt add a heavy burden to any loss, yet it is almost impossible not to wonder: If I'd been more careful; If I'd acted nicer; If only I'd done more. Such feelings are not unusual, but they do not necessarily reflect the true situation.

> Old Baxter-dog is gone — he died at the vet's and we didn't even know he was really sick. It was just that he hadn't been racing around much lately, chasing after me, barking hello. I guess it's my fault for not noticing. Maybe if I'd been paying more attention, not staying after school to play basketball — I could have spent more time with him.

Being angry at times is also not unusual: Why did you go off and leave me? How could you do this to me? Questions like these are part of the anger that comes from shock. They are natural reactions, but they can add to the load of guilt: I shouldn't be feeling this way.

> I can't believe Baxter's gone. He wasn't *that* old and he didn't act sick. Dammit Baxter, why'd you have to go get sick and die — didn't you *know* I need you?

Denial is a way to delay the necessary acceptance of the situation: When I wake up in the morning the newspaper will say it was all a mistake. He'll be there when I get home tonight. If I truly promise never to be so careless again, then I'll find what I lost.

> I just can't believe Baxter's really gone. I keep looking for him when I get up and when I come home from school, and I know it's dumb but I keep thinking I should go over to the animal hospital and maybe then I'll find out it's all a mistake.

Depression is a very natural part of grief. It is normal to withdraw, to be unhappy, to feel that life is empty, that you'll never want to do anything again.

> Baxter was special. When we first moved here he was the only friend I had. And when I did begin to go off and do things, he was always waiting, grinning, wagging his tail, glad to see me come home. And when I had things to talk over he always listened to

me—which is more than I can say for some of my other friends. He was always there. And now he isn't. And I feel like there's a great big hole in my life—in me.

Continued writing, exploring feelings, remembering, can, little by little, help to work through initial shock and pain.

Today Mom and I got to talking about when Baxter was a puppy and some of the funny things he did and we got to laughing and I said we shouldn't be laughing. But Mom said why not? We have sad memories but we have lots, lots more happy memories. And then we both started to cry but Mom said do you remember when you were little how Baxter would howl whenever you cried and then Mom and I were laughing and crying at the same time. Baxter would've loved it.

When we cry. There is a benefit for people in the act of crying.

> *Some people find it difficult to cry, while others find it easy and automatic.... However, tears are usually a necessary release with a language all their own, appearing when we are overwhelmed with feelings that words cannot describe. Tears are actually helpful, a very real part of the cleansing and healing process.*
>
> —Cheryl A. Kilbourn
> *For the Love of Princess—*
> *Surviving the Loss of Your Pet**

Intense feelings may make you cry. Writing about intense feelings may make you cry.

The last time I cried was _____

I cried because _____

These things make me cry: _____

Discuss how you feel about crying, when you cry, when people around you cry.

---

*Kilbourn, Cheryl A. *For the Love of Princess—Surviving the Loss of Your Pet.* Beaverton, Oreg.: Princess Publishing, 1987. P. 85.

Tears fall, no matter how we try to check them, and by being shed they ease the soul.

—Seneca
Letters

"It opens the lungs, washes the countenance, exercises the eyes, and softens down the temper," said Mr. Bumble. *"So cry away."*

—Charles Dickens
Oliver Twist

❑   ❑   ❑

CONCLUSION

Strong emotion, whatever the cause, needs to be expressed. Better, though, that it is expressed in a way that will not lead to hurt, misunderstanding, or self-reproach. The surest confidant and safety valve is the journal. Writing in detail about any happening that ignites strong feelings relieves the pressure, lessens the pain, and, with continued writing, gives perspective. It is in the emotional release of cathartic writing that the journal proves itself our most helpful, sympathetic, and understanding friend.

POINTS TO REMEMBER

- Your journal is the place for honest expression of feelings.

- Write quickly about emotional experiences without judging or editing.

- You can trust your journal to keep your secrets until you wish to share them with others.

- Strong feelings can boil over without your meaning for them to. A journal is your safety valve.

- Writing in a journal releases pain, anger, and hurt in a safe way.

- Looking at an emotional experience later can help you find perspective and understanding.

- Highly emotional joyful experiences written in your journal are preserved to delight in again.

- A journal is a safe place to explore deep feelings.

- Writing from another person's point of view can give you new insight.

- Fear is a natural emotion that belongs to all of us. Writing about fear helps diffuse and conquer it.

- A journal is the understanding friend who is always there for you.

SUGGESTED READING

Nonfiction

Kilbourn, Cheryl A. *For the Love of Princess—Surviving the Loss of Your Pet*. Beaverton, Oreg.: Princess Publishing, 1987.

Krementz, Jill, ed. *How It Feels When a Parent Dies*. New York: Alfred A. Knopf, 1981.

_____. *How It Feels When Parents Divorce*. New York: Alfred A. Knopf, 1984.

Quackenbush, Jamie, and Denise Graveline. *When Your Pet Dies*. New York: Simon & Schuster, 1985.

Richter, Elizabeth. *Losing Someone You Love: When a Brother or Sister Dies*. New York: Putnam, 1986.

Sternberg, Frankie, and Barbara Sternberg. *If I Die and When I Do: Exploring Death with Young People*. The Transformation Series. Englewood Cliffs, N.J.: Prentice-Hall, 1980.

Fiction

Bergstrom, Corinne. *Losing Your Best Friend*. New York: Human Sciences Press, 1980. When she loses her best friend to a new girl, a third grader first suffers, then learns to adjust her life.

Bulla, Clyde Robert. *The Cardboard Crown*. New York: Crowell, 1984. The life of an eleven-year-old farm boy is changed through his steadfast friendship for a young stranger from the city. For younger and middle-grade children.

_____. *Dexter*. New York: Crowell, 1973. The story of two friends, parted by circumstances and distance, and the promise they keep between them. For younger and middle-grade children.

Carrick, Carol. *The Accident*. New York: Seabury Press, 1976. After his dog is hit and killed by a truck, Christopher must deal with his own feelings of depression and guilt.

Cole, Sheila R. *Meaning Well*. New York: Franklin Watts, 1974. A sixth grader learns the meaning of friendship too late to help a classmate who desperately needs a friend.

de Paola, Tomie. *Now One Foot, Now the Other*. New York: Putnam, 1981. Deepening understanding grows between a boy and his grandfather when their situations are reversed.

Dixon, Paige. *Skipper*. New York: Atheneum, 1979. Sequel to *May I Cross Your Golden River*. Skipper, still grieving for his brother Jordan, who has died, goes to look for his absentee father while keeping a journal in the form of letters to Jordan. For older readers.

Duncan, Lois. *A Gift of Magic*. Boston: Little, Brown, 1971. Family separation, sibling jealousy, and ESP cause problems and feelings of guilt for the main character when there is an accident. For older readers.

Fox, Paula. *One-eyed Cat*. New York: Bradbury Press, 1984. A young boy is haunted by the feeling that he has wounded a cat on the night he used an air rifle forbidden him by his father.

Glaser, Dianne. *The Diary of Trilby Frost*. New York: Holiday House, 1976. Growing up in rural Tennessee at the beginning of the 1900s, teenager Trilby records in her diary her growing realization that life continues even though her father, younger brother, and closest childhood friend die.

Greene, Constance. *Your Old Pal, Al*. New York: Viking, 1979. A story of anger and the repercussions of a sent letter that should have remained unsent. For middle-grade readers.

Hoban, Russell. *A Baby Sister for Frances*. New York: Harper & Row, 1964. A picture book story of sibling rivalry.

Paterson, Katherine. *Jacob Have I Loved*. New York: Crowell, 1980. Like Esau in the Bible, Sara Louise feels deprived of her birthright because of the attention paid to her beautiful twin, Caroline, and because of the money spent for Caroline's education but not for her own. For older readers.

Peck, Richard. *Father Figure*. New York: Viking, 1978. Following his mother's suicide and after eight years of being a substitute father to his younger brother, Jim Atwater has to become acquainted with and learn to accept his own long-absent father. For older readers.

_____. *Remembering the Good Times*. New York: Delacorte, 1985. Friends become close friends as they grow from childhood into young adulthood. Then two of them must face the suicide of the third. For older readers.

Platt, Ken. *The Ape Inside Me*. New York: Lippincott, 1979. As a way of dealing with his anger, the main character gives that anger an identity of its own.

Smith, Doris Buchanan. *A Taste of Blackberries*. New York: Crowell, 1973. When Jamie dies in a sudden tragedy, a friend, who is the first-person narrator of the story, must find a way to bear his grief and his guilty feeling that somehow he might have saved Jamie. For middle-grade readers and older.

Stolz, Mary. *What Time of Night Is It?* New York: Harper & Row, 1981. A family comes to terms with themselves and their lives after the mother walks out.

Varley, Susan. *Badger's Parting Gifts.* New York: Lothrop, Lee & Shepard, 1984. The low-key mood is reminiscent of *The Wind in the Willows* in this handling of the death of a friend that emphasizes memories rather than sadness. A picture book for all ages.

Viorst, Judith. *The Tenth Good Thing about Barney.* New York: Atheneum, 1975. Dealing with the death of his cat Barney, the main character makes a list of the good things about the cat. The list becomes a tribute to a friend. A picture book for all ages.

CHAPTER 10

The Fantasy Journal

Vitality — that is the test [of fantasy]; and, whatever its components, mere truth is not necessarily one of them.

—Kenneth Grahame
Introduction to *A Hundred Fables of Aesop*

INTRODUCTION

A child's mind develops and grows as his or her body develops and grows. We sometimes forget this, expecting a child to have an understanding of the world as advanced as that of an adult — an adult who is frustrated because the child makes the wrong decision, or thinks things through with his or her own brand of logic.

In the beginning we are concerned only with ourselves, learning to understand ourselves better. As we grasp this concept, we start to understand others, relate to those around us, become a part of a larger world. But we never stop developing that interior landscape. We retreat there often, even as "mature" adults.

The journal is an invaluable tool to aid in developing one's inner resources: healthy emotions, self-confidence, positive feelings, creativity, intuition, and imagination.

It is this development of the imagination that lifts us above the level of worker ants. Dictators, who train the people under them to follow orders and to act without questioning, work hard to eliminate people of imagination who dare to speak out. As we saw in the late 1980s, these people go underground and continue to write and communicate in secret. It is impossible to completely destroy a people's imagination.

Studies of people imprisoned for long periods of time, especially in isolation, show that the prisoners who survive are those who keep up a vigorous fantasy life. Pianists practice in their minds, fingering their laps or the floor. They compose or play concerts daily. Writers create novels, write them in detail, commit them to memory in order to place them on paper when they are released.

As a rule, we call on our ability to fantasize without thinking about it. We do it to eliminate boredom or pass the time of day. Sometimes we use our fantasy life to escape, and, within reason, this is healthy. Only when fantasy replaces reality are we in trouble, dubbed psychotic by society. Using fantasy to escape is automatic, though. Seldom do we get ourselves in a mess and say, "Hold on here, I'd better have a fantasy to get myself out of this."

We must find time for a fantasy life. Think of it as playtime, recess, for our minds. The suggestions offered here can be expanded, added to, and adapted to the individuals who are using them. The main goal is to have fun daydreaming. But all parts of a fantasy represent some part of the dreamer. In a time of reflection or self-inspection, one can reread fantasies and ask these questions:

- Why did I choose this fantasy?

- Why this setting, this place?

- Why these characters?

- How does this fantasy relate to my real life?

- What emotions are in this fantasy?

- Did some emotion, state of mind, generate this fantasy? Do I still feel this way?

Choose one fantasy. Let the characters in the fantasy dialogue with each other or with the real you.

Analyzing one's fantasies is never necessary, however. It may be enough to have the fantasy, write it down, and forget it. Go on to another daydream. But if wondering why contributes to understanding oneself, it may be useful and fun.

PURPOSES AND AIMS

- To enjoy thinking about what might happen without needing for it to really happen

- To become more creative and expand our imaginations

- To learn to use fantasy for problem solving, rehearsing future behavior, and disempowering people

- To escape boredom and have fun writing about ourselves in a fanciful way

FANTASIES ABOUT THE PERSONAL YOU

A fairy godmother grants you three wishes. Choose them spontaneously — you may be granted three more tomorrow. What three would you wish today? Make these big wishes, not just for a toy you want or for things. After you have listed the three, look at them. Discuss with yourself why you chose these three. If you asked for a million dollars, why do you want or need a lot of money? What would you do with it? Are any of these wishes really possible? What could you do to get any of these wishes without wishing?

Change yourself. If you could change three things about yourself, what would they be? After you have decided, write why you want or need to change any of these things? One cannot change physical characteristics except by plastic surgery, but are there other ways to change these three things? For instance, if you said, "Change the way I dress," but you realize that takes money you don't have, could you learn to sew? Weight lifting and other physical fitness programs can change your image.

Catalog orders. What if you could order a new you from the Sears catalog? Write a letter putting in the order. Have fun doing it.

Put in an additional order for the ideal friend. What would he or she be like? Make this a detailed order. Write down not just looks, but also talents and personality traits.

Order something for your mother or father or another family member. For example, you might order more time for your mother so she will be less stressed and less angry.

Wants. Make a list of your wants, not needs. You can have anything you want on this list.

Make a list of why you think you might not get these things or why you haven't had these things before.

- I'm not good enough.

- My mother says I don't need it.

- I never get what I want.

- I don't ever know what I want.

- I don't have enough money.

- I don't deserve this.

Draw a large gray bubble around this list. Close your eyes. See this bubble float away. It goes farther and farther away from you — over the treetops, over roofs nearby, up, up, up, toward the clouds, away, out of sight, beyond the horizon.

List the things you want again. Cut out a picture, or draw a picture of each thing or the thing you want most. Write a passage in which you get what you want. How did you get it? Did it arrive in a package at your door? Did you have to work for it? Save for it? Did you get it for your birthday? Write down how you enjoy having it.

Going places. Make a list of places you'd like to visit. Choose one. Write about your going there. What does it look like? Smell like? What sounds do you hear there? What things do you do there? Do you bring back any souvenirs? Remember you can go any place you like. There is no limit to your imagination.

REWRITING THE PAST

Using fantasy to rewrite the past can have both positive and negative effects. You might think of an argument you had and lost. In your mind, or your journal, you'd replay the dialogue, and this time you'd say all the right things and win. This may be satisfying just to rid yourself of the leftover anger you have, but it won't really win the argument. You might pick a part of your life, go back, and live it over again. Novelists do this all the time. We make things better, change the outcome, and perhaps feel better because of the vicarious experience of getting to do something we felt we had been deprived of. If this type of recalling and rewriting the past becomes an obsession or an exercise in self-pity, or if it becomes confused with what really happened, it can be negative.

If you had your life, so far, to live over again, what would you do differently? What would you keep the same? Make a list of things you'd do.

- I'd let my hair grow and never cut it.

- I'd write my grandmother every week.

- I'd tell Mr. Langston that the reason I don't read more is that I can't. I'd tell him that I see the letters all funny, that I'm not lazy.

- I wouldn't give up my piano lessons, and I'd practice more.

- I'd try more new things. When Rose asked me to go horseback riding, I wouldn't tell her I was afraid of horses. I'd try it.

- I'd help out at home more without complaining.

- I'd save half my allowance every week. Then I could go shopping with Susan without being embarrassed.

- I'd take that job delivering papers in our neighborhood.

- I'd try out for the school play.

- I'd tell Ms. Shepard I don't understand the math problems rather than flunk the test and let her think I'm dumb.

- I'd hold our old cat Fizzy more and pet her before she gets old and dies.

- I wouldn't tell my sister she has an ugly nose. I'd make her a list of all the famous people I know with big noses.

Look at your list. There will be some things you can't do over or take back. Are there any you can still do? Try again? Think about these. Write about any of the things on your list. Write a news story. Write a dialogue in which you do what you say you'd have done.

MARY JOHNSON TERRIFIC IN SCHOOL PLAY

When the last curtain rang down Saturday night, the audience gave Mary Johnson a standing ovation. She had everyone crying and laughing all evening with her performance. Mary tells us she almost didn't try out for the play. It's hard to imagine anyone else in this role. It seems to have been written for her. She says she'll continue with drama, since she's been bitten by the acting bug.

Janie:	(Comes in crying and throws herself down on the bed) I could just die! No one asked me out again this weekend. It's because I have such a big nose. I know it is.
Me:	Janie, that's not true. Lots of people have big noses. Look at Barbra Streisand. She has a huge nose.
Janie:	But she's a movie star. She's famous.

Me: She wasn't always famous. What if she'd have said, I can't be a star, I'm ugly?

Janie: If Mom and Dad would let me have it fixed I'd be popular. I told them I'd work and pay for half of it.

Me: What if you had your nose fixed and still no one asked you out?

Janie: Thanks a lot, Carol. You just don't understand. You got Mom's nose. You're really pretty. And next year you'll get tons of dates. I'll have to stay home and watch you going out. (Starts to cry)

Me: Janie, do you want to know the truth?

Janie: (Crying) No!

Me: I'm going to tell you anyway. Because you think you're ugly, you keep your head down all the time. You act shy. If a guy tried to talk to you, he'd have a terrible time getting your attention. You have a beautiful smile. Think of the money Mom and Dad have already spent getting your teeth straightened. If you'd stand up straight and smile and look guys right in the eye, they'd smile back and want to get to know you better. What if Barbra Streisand went around with one of those big hats she wears over her face? Hiding behind it?

Janie: (Trying to laugh) That's silly.

Me: I'll tell you what. Try my idea. If it doesn't work, I'll spend some of my savings to buy you a big hat with roses all over it. You can carry it around and peep over it at guys.

Janie: (Laughing) I know you're right, Carol. I'll try. But have your money ready in case it doesn't work.

USING FANTASY IN YOUR LIFE

Some of the most fascinating things you do are in your head. You win lotteries and contests, ice skate in the Olympics, run and win marathons, explore unknown planets, and swim underwater to a hidden city and become their king or queen. We are exotic spies or successful detectives; we solve mysteries, escaping peril in the nick of time. Unlike real life, this inner life is very satisfying since we are always beautiful, thin enough, tall enough, and have straight noses and curly hair. We always win. We say the right things at the right time, and people are amazed. They admire us, praise us, love us.

Rehearsing future behavior. You can use fantasy to rehearse future behavior. You have finally gotten the date of the century. You plan how you'll dress and act, what you'll talk about, and what you can order for dinner and still eat gracefully. Perhaps the evening doesn't work out exactly as you'd planned, but by then the fantasy is forgotten, real life has set in, and you understand that very little works out exactly as planned.

Today's the big sports event. You want to win. Imagine yourself playing the game, participating in the event. You are incredible. All your practicing pays off. Write about your being the star in detail. How do you feel? What is happening around you? Describe the event or the game. Detail your part of it. See yourself doing your best.

You are very shy. But you have to ask for a job you want. Imagine yourself going through the steps that lead up to the interview. How would you dress? How would you act when you got there? What could you do to make yourself more confident? Before you go, brag (to yourself) about your skills, the skills you have for this job. Exaggerate about how wonderful you are. Say why this person needs you on this job. Exaggerate some incredible things that will happen if you're in this job. You save the day for your employer. You save the whole business. Now say what your skills are without bragging. Write down why you want the job and why the person should hire you. Write a dialogue between yourself and the person who is interviewing you.

You:	Good morning. I've come to interview for....
Interview Person:	Thank you for coming. I need someone in this job right away.
You:	I think I'm the person you need.
IP:	What makes you think that?
You:	You've seen my application. But let me review my skills. I can....
IP:	I have several people who have your same qualifications. Why should I choose you over them?
You:	I get along well with people. I'm not afraid to work hard. Here are some ideas I've had on how to improve the service here. I asked five people what they liked or disliked about your business. Here is what I'd do about what they disliked. Perhaps you could include what they liked in your advertising.
IP:	You seem to have done a lot of thinking about working here.

You: I would like to work here. I think I'd be happy here. When I made a list of places I'd like to work, your business was at the top of the list.

IP: I like my employees to be happy. I think you're right. I think you're the person I'm looking for. You're hired. When can you start?

Problem solving. Fantasy is useful as a tool for problem solving. You can imagine yourself living out a situation for an alternate number of choices that you have. If you choose option A, this will happen, but if you choose option B, here is what life will be like. If I go to college I will become a lawyer and become famous for my cases, but if I go to Hollywood and wait tables, perhaps I'll be discovered and star in movies instead. Many people follow the less realistic choice, following a fantasy, but after a few years, they recognize it as a fantasy and return to a more likely career, based on hard work. Life, in a moment of whimsy, may see the lawyer take a part as an extra in a Perry Mason film, be discovered, and then be hired for a larger part in another show.

Think of a problem you are having. Use fantasy to project yourself into the situation, trying different solutions to the problem. Through your writing live out the result of each choice. Which fantasy do you like best? Perhaps this is the real solution to try. It may not turn out just as you'd imagined. Your choice may even be a mistake, but the only way to learn that is by trying it out.

Ray Bradbury has said that life is trying things to see if they work. By using fantasy and writing down how something *might* work, you will feel more comfortable trying it.

If you are a pessimist by nature, you can even write down a "worst-case scenario." Maybe by the time you are finished, you'll be laughing and can see that life does tend to equal things out.

If I try out for the basketball team, I'll fall on my face every time I try to dribble the ball down the floor. Then during a big game I'll get the ball and throw it and it'll hit Jerry Carter in the face and break his glasses. He'll have just done a cartwheel so he'll fall and break his arm, so of course he'll hold me responsible. He'll hate me and never ask me out. Then the coach won't let me go to the locker room even after Jerry is carried off to the hospital. He'll say he doesn't have enough players as it is. I'll fall the next time I have the ball and break my leg and I'll end up at the hospital, too. Because I break my leg I won't get to go to the spring dance, but because I wanted to go only with Jerry Carter, who cares? But ... wouldn't it be funny if while Jerry and I are both in the hospital, we're taken to therapy at the same time and we talk and he discovers that off the basketball floor I'm a pretty neat person and he asks me for a date if I promise not to ever play basketball again?

USING FANTASY TO GAIN PERSONAL POWER

Children, teens, and adults sometimes find themselves stuck in a position where they are powerless. This is frustrating no matter what one's age. When you become aware of lack of power, it seems that everyone is running your life except you. And often this is true. Perhaps you enjoy reading books where main characters have power, do things, even win over adults.

We have all experienced as children imagining we are adopted; surely we were left on the doorstep; these can't be my parents; or I have no parents. Father is dead. Mother is on an extended vacation. No one will tell you what you should do, can do, can't do, need to do.

> My mother is deaf. She can't hear anything I say to her. She is blind, too. She can't see anything I am doing. I did this to her. I had this magic potion. I gave it to her. I can take it back anytime I like, but right now, she doesn't even know or care where I am or what I'm doing.

This type of fantasy is usually harmless. It is your way of gaining power, even temporarily.

This type of imagining is often useful, however, to help us forget, ignore, laugh at, or take a vacation from someone real, someone we can't eliminate from our lives right now, even if we want to.

Disempowering techniques. There is someone in your life who is giving you a bad time, unfairly. You spend too much time worrying about this person, but you can't do anything about it at this time. Perhaps it is a bully. Perhaps a parent is being unfair, or a teacher. The best thing to do would be to laugh at or forget this person, but you can't seem to do that. In the book *Oliver Dibbs and the Dinosaur Cause*, Oliver is having trouble with Lester, a bully. He makes a list of funny or disastrous situations to put Lester in. He can't do this, but he can imagine it. After he makes the list, he laughs so much that he isn't angry at Lester any more.

Make a list of things you can do to the person who is bothering you. Concentrate on making them funny rather than mean or violent. You don't want to hurt this person, but you want him or her to have less power over you.

- I will send him on a hundred-year trip exploring the universe.

- I will put her in a swamp where every step is hard because she might fall into quicksand, but she has to hurry because crocodiles are chasing her.

- He hates noise. I'll surround him with the loudest football crowd ever at the most exciting Super Bowl ever. Every time he moves his seat, the crowd will follow.

- She hates my music. She won't let me play it even in my room. She will have an aura that activates boom boxes. Every person she gets close to has one. Her aura will turn them on full blast so she is surrounded by rock music at the time. She will beg me to get this stopped and let me play my radio and I won't turn it up so loud this time.

- I'll wrap him in flypaper and every time he moves he'll get more stuck and it'll take him ten years to get loose.

- She'll work at a department store and be in charge of returns and all day every day for a hundred years she'll have to listen to people saying why they're bringing something back.

All powerful. Here comes that fairy godmother again. She has made you all-powerful. You can do anything you want to do with your life, your time, the people around you. What would you do? Would you use your power for personal gain or would you improve the world? Maybe you would just improve your life.

You are principal of your school. What would you do to improve your school, to make it a more stimulating and enjoyable place, for students? You are president of the United States. What would you do?

DREAMS, TIME FANTASIES, AND CREATIVE FANTASIES

Dreams are a type of fantasy life. Dreams are influenced by what is happening in our real lives, or what has happened in the past, but we are seldom in control of the story. In an advanced stage of daydreaming, a fantasy may take over and dip into our unconscious, but we are still somewhat in charge.

Write down your dreams for at least a week. Instead of taking each dream literally, look for these things in your dreams.

1. What type of thing do you usually dream about? People? Animals? Houses? Adventures?

2. Do you see any patterns in your dreams? For instance, do you often dream about driving a car, exploring a house, hiking on the same mountain trail? Do you often dream about the same person?

3. If you often dream about being out of control in some way—skiing too fast, driving too fast, falling—can you relate this to your life? Do you feel out of control in your life? Can you discuss why with yourself?

4. Can you discover where a particular pattern of dreams is coming from? For instance, if you dream about one person all the time, is this person a part of your life, or has this person left your life for some reason?

Daddy, I dream about you all the time. I guess I am worried about you. I KNOW I am worried about you. I still can't understand why you left us, but would you just write to me, tell me you're all right? Last night I dreamed you were in a car wreck. Night before last I dreamed you fell off a mountain. Last week was the worst. I was running after you and you kept getting farther and farther away. I couldn't catch up to you. It would help so much if you could just write and say you're okay. You don't have to explain why you left, just tell me you're all right.

Knowing why you are dreaming a certain thing may not solve the problem, but writing about it will help you come to terms with why you keep repeating the dream. Often things we don't want to think about in the daytime come out in dreams at night. Facing these problems and writing about them can help us understand them, even if we are powerless at the time to improve the situation.

What if you didn't need to sleep? What would you do with all the extra time? Make a list or write some dialogue, or both.

What if you looked in the mirror and there were two of you? What would you assign your clone to do? Make a list of all the uses you can find for this clone.

You visit the doctor and she gives you the sad news that you have only six months to live. But you won't be sick during that time. You say, "I won't let this be a sad time. Here's what I'll do." Money is no problem. You can have all the money you need and do anything you want to do in this six months. What would you do?

You are riding a carousel. Suddenly your horse takes off and flies away from the carnival. Where does it go? Maybe it can go anyplace you want to go. What will you do while you're there? Can you bring it back, hide it in your garage, and go someplace again? Any time you like? Would you tell anyone about it? Take anyone along?

You find what looks like an ordinary pencil. But little by little you find that anything you draw becomes real. How would you use this pencil? Protect it? Could it be used for both good and bad? How would you discover that this pencil is magic? The pencil doesn't have an eraser. You can't take back anything you draw, so be careful.

You are graffiti on a wooden fence. What would you say about yourself in just a few words?

You go up in a hot-air balloon that is on a tether, so it won't go anyplace. You are alone. You enjoy being so high, looking down at your town, the people on the ground. Suddenly a strong gust of wind breaks the balloon loose. You drift away. Where do you go? Can you control the balloon? Or do you have to go wherever it takes you? How does it feel to be so high? What do you see? How do you feel? Write your adventure.

TREASURE HUNTING

You go exploring in your attic. There are stacks of boxes, tons of old things. You come across a marvelous treasure. What is it? What would you do with it?

You are deep-sea diving on your vacation. You enjoy being underwater. You swim and swim. You see many varieties of tropical fish. You go deeper and deeper. Suddenly you come upon a solid gold chest. There is a piece of rusted iron near by. You take a tool and break open the chest. What is in it? What would you do with it? It may not be what you imagined before you open it. It may not be money, gold coins, jewels, but.... Will it make you famous? Cause you problems? Make your life better, more interesting? Will there be some magic to it?

Draw a treasure map in your journal. Cut out or draw things you'd like and place them along the way in the path the map follows. You can make this map for the year that's coming up. The treasures are the things you'd like to have this coming year. The big treasure at the end is the biggest or the best thing you'd like to have this year.

There is something magic about actually writing down what you'd like or need. Writing it and seeing it helps you get it. Look at this treasure map often to remind yourself of what it is you set out to find. Travel over the trail from thing to thing, seeing yourself receive them. If you like, you can make a large treasure map, identical to the one in your journal, and hang it on the wall in your room. That way you can see it every day.

CONCLUSION

We must believe in fantasy in order to make it useful in our lives. We must believe that using our imaginations is important, that we need to be creative in thought as well as in deed. We must stop thinking that daydreaming is a waste of time. We must remind ourselves that fantasy is harmless, a way to rest and eliminate stress from our busy lives. After all, one of the few real freedoms we have left is daydreaming; one of the few places we can truly be free is in our minds.

POINTS TO REMEMBER

- Imagination lifts you above the level of a worker ant.

- Imagination sets you free.

- Writing about your fantasies in a journal is a healthy way to escape when the world is too much for you to handle.

- Practicing using your imagination makes you more creative.

- You can use fantasy to rewrite and relive the past in a positive and satisfying way.

- By recording and studying your dreams in your journal you can make discoveries about yourself.

- You need never be bored with an active imagination and your journal as companions.

CHAPTER 11

The All-About-People Journal

Folks are better than angels.
—Edward Thompson Taylor, Boston minister
(when on his deathbed his friends said he would
soon be with the angels)

The mind of the people is like mud,
From which arise strange and beautiful things.
—W. J. Turner
"Talking with Soldiers"

INTRODUCTION

No man is an island. We have all heard this statement, and we have to admit it's true. We live on this planet with others. We don't know all of them, of course. We couldn't know all of them. But in many ways we are related and linked to all other human beings. What they do affects us. What we do affects them. And while we never want to forget that each of us is unique, like snowflakes, we can understand ourselves better by studying and understanding others.

PURPOSES AND AIMS

- To expand on the people-in-your-life section in chapter 3

- To think about all the people who influence us

- To think about and identify relationships

- To enjoy people's idiosyncracies and the human zoo around us

- To learn from people around us

LINKING

Listing links. List the people to whom you are linked. This would include family, friends, teachers, ministers, rabbis, and perhaps neighbors and a few people in stores where you go all the time. If you mow a yard or shovel snow for one person on a regular basis, you are linked to that person. If your class visits in a nursing home and you always visit one elderly person, you have a link to that person.

Choose one person on your list and discuss your relationship. Look at the little things that tie you together. Don't forget the negative as well as the positive. If some bully at school steals your lunch money two or three times a week, you are linked to that person. You have let him or her have power over you. Why have you done this? What could you do about it?

Answer some or all of these questions when thinking about a linking relationship:

- What do I get out of this link? (Go beyond money.)

- What do I put in?

- What does the other person get? Put in?

- What needs does this relationship satisfy for me?

- Have you ever had a fight with this person?

- How am I important to this other person?

- How is this person important to me?

For three years I have mowed Mrs. Dickens's yard, and in the winter I shovel her driveway and walks. I earn part of my spending money doing this. But Mrs. Dickens has become my friend. I always talk to her for a few minutes when I collect my money. Sometimes she gives me a soft drink or a cup of cocoa. One time, when I had a fight with my mother, I needed to tell someone. I told Mrs. Dickens. She helped me see my mother's side of the argument. I have never been a mother but Mrs. Dickens has. One time when I found out Mrs. Dickens was sick, I went to the store for her. Then I made her a cup of tea and put away the groceries. I guess she is like an adopted grandmother for me. Both my grandmothers live in another state, so I don't get to see them often. My mother is allergic to cats, so I can't have one. I have adopted Mrs. Dickens's cat, Oliver, too. She said she got that name from a book I might like to read someday.

Dialogue with someone with whom you have had a fight, but put yourself inside the other person to write the conversation.

Losing links. Occasionally we have to give up a person in our life, a link in our personal chain. Sometimes — usually — it takes time to replace or close up that link. What people have you had to give up in your life who were important to you? Discuss the relationship you had with this person, then the feelings you had when the relationship broke apart. What made the link break? Was anyone or both of you at fault, or did the person move or die? Have you ever had a friend who changed so much you couldn't be friends anymore?

Have a dialogue with or write a letter to a person you have had to give up.

Dear Grandpa,

I feel cheated because I never got to meet you. My father says you collected stamps, and so do I. We could trade if you were alive today. Did you have any rare stamps? I wish my father could have had your collection, but he said you had to sell it to pay some bills. So maybe you had an upside-down Jenny or something great like that.

When our class went to the nursing home, I talked to people there until I found a man who collects stamps. Now I go to visit him every week on my own. We look at our collections and sometimes trade. He's helped me learn a lot.

Would you mind if I pretended he was my grandpa? It won't make me forget you.

Love,
Bobby

Cementing links. Think about relationships in your life. How long has it been since you:

• hugged your mother/father/sister/brother?

• told someone you loved him or her?

- took time to listen to a friend's problem?

- knocked on your brother's or sister's bedroom door before entering?

- hogged the bathroom?

- made a mess and didn't clean it up?

- cleaned up a mess without asking who made it?

- said "thank you" for a little thing someone did for you?

Picturing links. Draw a chain that pictures the people to whom you are linked. Are some of the links bigger than others? Are some fragile or strained? Are some closed tighter than others?

PEOPLE ARE FUNNY

Many of us like to go to places like zoos, animal parks, and oceanariums. But when you stop and think about it, aren't people really the most fascinating animals of all? We are funny, serious, strange, beautiful, ugly, tall, short, fat, and skinny. We do good things, bad things, weird things. Take a look in the *Guinness Book of World Records* if you have any doubts.

In 1900 a man walked on his hands for 871 miles. He walked from Vienna to Paris averaging 1.58 miles per hour. Another man set the record in 1985 for jumping on a pogo stick 130,077 times. Can you beat that? Would you want to? How would you like to lie on a bed of nails for three hundred hours? You'd have to do that to break the record. Do you like to camp? A man in India camped by the roadside, in one place, never moving, for twenty-two years. If you played hopscotch for more than 102 hours, you could break that record. Or you could carry a fresh egg in a dessert spoon for over twenty-eight miles in less than four and a half hours. Could you balance more than seven golf balls on top of each other? The same man set the record with six in 1977.

There's a woman who hasn't cut her hair since 1971. It's ten feet nine inches long. It takes her four hours to shampoo it. I'll bet you like to iron. If you stayed at the ironing board for over 128 hours you would set a new record.

Why do people do such things? Good question. Maybe they need to be famous, or maybe they do it just for fun.

WEIRD PEOPLE

Your idiosyncracies. What is the strangest thing you ever did? Write about it. Why did you do it? Did anything good or bad come of doing it?

Strange ancestors. What is the strangest thing anyone in your family ever did? Have there been any stories handed down in your family about strange ancestors?

Strange friends. What is the strangest thing anyone you know ever did? Anyone in your school?

Strange collections. Do you know anyone who has a strange collection? What is it?

> I have a friend who collects Dracula stuff. He has a lot of books about Dracula and Dracula posters from movies and books. He has a closet full of clothes he calls his Dracula wardrobe. Every Halloween he dresses like Dracula. He wears a formal black suit, a black cape with red lining, and a black top hat. He combs his hair the way he thinks Dracula would comb it. He even had a dentist make him fangs to fit in his mouth like a retainer. Sometimes he goes for a walk at 2:00 a.m. dressed like the Count. He stands on a hill and lets the wind blow his cloak. What would people think if they saw him there in the middle of the night?

Write a piece that states your thoughts about why you think people do strange things.

IMPORTANT PEOPLE IN YOUR LIFE OVER TIME

Teachers. Make a list of all the teachers you remember having. Pick out your favorite and write about him or her. Why did you like this teacher? What were his or her best and worst traits? Which teacher helped you learn the most — and how? Which teacher do you think had the most influence on you? Why? What did you do or how did you improve yourself because of this person? Do you like men or women teachers best, or do you have no preference? If you have a preference, say why.

Think of some teachers or coaches you had who were not in school — piano teachers, soccer coaches, swim team coaches, art or writing teachers. Choose the one you think had the most influence on you and describe this person. Talk about why he or she influenced you.

Authors. Make a list of your favorite books of all time. Certainly you enjoyed the story in these books or you wouldn't have listed them. But all books have authors. Do any of the authors of these books stick in your mind? Can you say that any special author influenced you through his or her book, through something he or she said in the book? The story? The characters? Events that happened in the book?

> When I read Judy Blume's books, I remember that everyone has trouble growing up. It's not just me. Everyone worries about looks and pimples. I was worried about how much my body was changing and how fast. When I read *Are You There, God? It's Me, Margaret*, I knew lots of girls worried about these things. What I was thinking about was normal. It was all right to think about it. I stopped feeling so much alone. I wrote her a letter to tell her I liked the book. She didn't write me a personal letter, but she sent me a list of her other books that I might like. I have read all of them. I have learned a lot about myself by reading her books.

People you have admired but never known. Make a list of people you have admired over the years. You need not have known these people. Perhaps you have always admired Thomas Edison because he invented so many things. Maybe you always wanted to be a great baseball pitcher and you admire Orel Hershiser. You are a fan of Teddy Roosevelt or Abraham Lincoln. Your favorite music to play is Mozart. You've learned a lot from him. You love animals and wish you could live your life like Jane Goodall has. What animal would you study first?

You would like to explore the moon and you admire Neil Armstrong, the first person on the moon. You would like to be a movie star or a rock singer. Who is a favorite that you admire?

Choose one on your list and read about that person's life. Is your life anything like his or hers? What personality traits does this person have? Do you have any of those same traits? Could you develop some? Imagine yourself inside that person for a day or week or year. What would your life be like? Write about your life as that person. Write about your life as *you* following in that person's footsteps.

TAKE YOUR OWN CENSUS

Every ten years the government counts people and asks them questions. Conduct a census at your house, using the following questions:

- How many children in your house? How many boys? Girls?

- Who is the oldest child? Youngest?

- How many meals a year are fixed in your kitchen?

- What are your family's favorite meals? Least favorite?

- How many slices of pizza has your family eaten this year? Slices of bread? Gallons of milk? Cans of pop?

- Who has the strangest hobby at your house?

- Who has traveled the most? To the strangest place? The farthest place?

- What was your favorite vacation? Worst? Longest?

- How many national parks has your family visited? Caves? States? How many states has your family lived in?

- When did you have the most pets? The strangest pet?

- Which cat or dog that you've had had the strangest trick or habit?

- What is the biggest house you've ever lived in? The smallest?

- How many personal computers are there in your house?

- Who is your oldest relative? Youngest?

- Who has the most books in his or her room? The most stuffed animals? The most tropical fish?

- How many bicycles at your house?

- What's the biggest yard you ever had? Yard with the most trees?

- What room has the most indoor plants? The most exotic?

- How many movies has your family seen this year? What was your favorite? Your family's favorite?

- Who in your family has read the most books this year?

- Who has watched the most television? How many hours, on average, per person?

- Who participates in the most sports? Who plays a sport you think is unique?

- What games does your family like to play? Which is the most popular?

- Who has played the most hours of games?

- Who has seen the most species of animals? Birds?

What other questions can you think of to ask about family? If other people in your class do a personal census, compare your family's results to theirs.

PEOPLE ADVICE

The people around you are always willing to give you advice. Check with some of the following people and ask them questions. What other people can you think of to interview?

Oldest. Interview the oldest person in your town or neighborhood. Ask this person what advice he or she could give you on living your life. Write what you think about taking this advice.

Librarian. Interview one of your city or school librarians. Ask him or her to make a list of the ten most important books that you should read during your lifetime. Put this list in your journal. Check off the book when you have read it. (You may have to wait until you are older to read some of the books.) Your school librarian might suggest the ten best books in your school library. You could start with these.

Physical education teacher or school nurse. Interview your PE teacher or the school nurse. Ask him or her to give you a list of lifelong habits you can adopt and specific things you can do to improve your health and nutrition. Put the list in your journal. Check them off as you do them. Are there some you can't do? Don't want to do? Why? Discuss why or why not.

Some health experts say we would be healthier if we all became vegetarians. That might be true, but I don't think I could give up hamburgers. And I like steaks, meatballs on my spaghetti, pepperoni on my pizza, and — well — you can see my dilemma. I believe in cow rights, but I think some animals are raised for food. I can have my mother buy beef that is raised in a healthy and humane way. And I guess I could eat more vegetarian meals. Now that I think about it, I do like macaroni and cheese and spinach lasagna and quiche. But please don't make me eat tofu. I know it's bean curd, but I agree with my cousin. He calls it bean turd.

Police officer. Interview a police officer. Ask him or her to tell you ten things you can do now to stay out of trouble your entire life. Discuss these things. Can you do them? Check off those you already do and the others as you do them.

Psychologist or counselor. Get a list of things you can do now to help you have a mentally healthy life. Ask about the ten most important mental health habits a person can aspire to. Discuss them. Why do you think these would help you live a better life? Are there any you have already adopted? Do you disagree with any items on the list? Can you add any? At the same time, ask for a list of ways to make and keep friends.

Principal. Ask your principal for a list of the most important things you can do to get a good education. Discuss these with yourself and your friends. Write your opinion of the list. Can you add anything to it?

Mayor or city council member. Find out what kinds of things someone your age can do to be a good citizen of your city or town. Make your own personal list from these suggestions. Check off those you do and keep tabs on how often you do them.

Ecologist. Ask someone who is involved with environmental issues what things you as an individual can do to help save Planet Earth. Make plans to do them. How will you go about doing each? Do you have a favorite cause? Why do you think it is important?
You may get the following suggestions and more:

- Recycle your family's newspaper, glass, and plastic.

- Help neighbors recycle paper. (It takes an entire forest — over 500,000 trees — to supply Americans with their Sunday newspapers every week.)

- Plant a tree. (The average American uses the equivalent of seven trees every year.)

- Cut up six-pack rings. (They have become hazards to ocean birds and other marine life. During a beach cleanup along three hundred miles of Texas shoreline in 1988, 15,600 plastic six-pack rings were found in three hours.)

- Don't buy anything that comes packaged in styrofoam. (Americans produce enough styrofoam cups every year to circle the earth 436 times. They won't go away. Five hundred years from now your cup will still be around.)

> To help save Planet Earth, I'm going to help my neighbors recycle newspapers. Things I'll need: A wagon. I could tie a box to my skateboard. Paper bags to put them in. A note to tell my neighbors when I'll pick up each week. If my town doesn't pick up newspapers to recycle, I'll find out where to take them. I'll ask my mom or dad to take me there once a week. I'll write my city council and ask them to help our city recycle. I'll write my newspaper and ask them to use recycled paper for our hometown paper.

CONCLUSION

We can use our journals to help us know and get along with the people around us. We can learn how to live together. Think of a huge chain circling the earth. You are one link in that chain. Your journal can help you think about being a stronger link. It can help you think of how to replace a link that has broken or fallen away. While each of us is an individual and wants to continue being a unique person all on our own, we can learn how to contribute individually to life on this earth. We can learn to make a difference so that others gain by and appreciate our efforts. Each individual makes a difference. What you do in your lifetime counts.

Our journals will help us appreciate people who are unique, those who may seem, at first meeting, to be strange or have weird habits. While you may not want to adopt any weird habits or dress in strange ways, you may grow to realize that it takes courage to stand on your own. It takes strength to not always follow a crowd.

Life alone on a desert island would be boring after a short time. We want to enjoy our companions and share our experiences. We want to learn how other people can enrich our lives and how we can enrich theirs.

POINTS TO REMEMBER

- You are linked to the people around you. A journal can help you explore these links.

- You can understand yourself better by studying and understanding others.

- The journal can help you find out who the people are who influence you, and how these people go about exerting this influence.

- The journal can help you discover how you relate to other people who are close to you.

- We learn from each other. Use your journal to discover how and what you have learned and what you are teaching.

- A journal can help you appreciate people who are unique.

- People are funny. Let your journal help you enjoy the human race.

Using Your Journal
to Practice Fiction

*Some things can only be said in fiction, but
that doesn't mean they aren't true.*

—Aaron Lathan
(from article in *Writers on Writing*)

INTRODUCTION

Most writers keep a journal. And most say they go back and find many ideas for fiction in their daily entries. The authors find that they always use their travel journals to remind them of settings they want to use in a story. The description for how the mountains of Tennessee look in autumn or the streets of London look shrouded with fog will be taken almost verbatim from a journal entry.

You will find that a lot of truth comes out when you write fiction. Feelings you have tucked away carefully can pour out through the supposed safety of writing fiction. If this happens, it needed to happen, of course. There is no way to truly hide hurt, disappointment, grief, and other realities. You can only suppress those feelings. Fiction writing is terrific therapy. You may be able to acknowledge the truth only when you are pretending it's fiction. But most of the time, accepting the truth makes you feel better or helps you heal, especially if it's an old truth or an ancient wound. Truths lie deep within, watching and waiting for a way to escape. A certain freedom comes with letting feelings out in safe and creative ways.

You can practice writing styles in your journal. You can write poetry, even if you have never done so before. Maybe it isn't even poetry, but you can call it that, since no one will ever see it (unless it truly is wonderful and you want to copy it and market it one day). You can write jingles and doggerel that please your ear or make you laugh.

You may also find some insight into a situation by fictionalizing a real event in your life. Having to write dialogue or thoughts from the viewpoint of other people may remind you of their feelings, strengths, and weaknesses.

You can write five-minute novels with *you* as the main character. You can go back and choose some of your fantasies or time travels and write them into five-minute romances, westerns, high-adventure novels, or science fiction. Fun is what we're talking about—the fun and vicarious experience of writing fiction. Live your fiction as you write it. Your life will never be dull again.

PURPOSES AND AIMS

- To find real-life events that can be expanded into story form

- To enjoy writing about yourself as the main character

- To uncover truths about yourself and others

- To entertain yourself in a creative manner

THE FIVE-MINUTE NOVEL WITH YOU AS MAIN CHARACTER

Fill out the character chart on pages 144-45. This is not serious or life-threatening, so be spontaneous. Give yourself a limited time, say fifteen minutes. Put down the first thing that comes to your mind. You can and will put down something different the next time you do this. Some of your answers will depend on where your life is on any given day. And some of them will depend on your mood. Maybe you're feeling silly. You make out a silly chart and write a silly novel. It's good therapy. Maybe you're in the mood to murder a certain individual. Here's your chance, and it's not even against the law. Fiction writers get even with every person who has ever hurt or offended them, usually without the offenders even knowing about it. But the author feels better for it. Through a piece of fiction you can often say, "I'm sorry, forgive me" or "Now I understand," even if some of the characters you write about are dead. A piece of fiction may be your only way to say thank you. And the gift of a story is one to be treasured.

Your novel. After you have finished filling out your chart look it over. What's the first idea that comes to your mind for a good story? Be spontaneous. There are dozens of stories in your chart. Pick one per novel. You may write as many novels as you like. Don't try to write more than one at a sitting, however. After you have found your idea, give yourself five, ten, fifteen minutes—a half hour at most—to write the story. The faster you write, the better the novel will be. This is a mini-novel, not one that's two hundred pages long. And remember, you aren't writing for publication here but for your own enjoyment.

CHARACTER CHART OF YOU
AS MAIN CHARACTER

Name:

Title for your life as a novel:

Metaphor of first impression of you (general) or your appearance (e.g., a sparrow, a cocker spaniel, a blender):

Relationship to other people in your life (e.g., ringmaster, servant, delivery boy):

Mental equipment:
    Brain power:
    Special knowledge or abilities:
    Real occupation:
    Fantasy occupation:
    Plan for future occupations:

Chief interests:

Pleasures:

Hobbies:

Last time you did one of these:

Phobias, fears, and frustrations:

If there were six of you—a collection—describe yourself (e.g., raft of survivors, a phlox of gardeners, a brood of pessimists):

Your life ambition:

Where did this come from (personal choice, external, etc.):

Best friend:

Best friend's description of you:

Best enemy:

Best enemy's description of you:

Character tag:

Strongest character trait:

Weakest character trait:

Character trait that gets you in the most trouble:

One-line characterization (e.g., She was a small gray pigeon of a woman who walked as if the world was carpeted):

Why you individualize your life (e.g., your dress—you wear hats all the time, maybe funny hats—your hairstyle—something creative or unusual you do with a piece of your time—you're a clown—you write thank-you letters to everyone you hear of who does something good):

Three wishes: 1.
             2.
             3.

Something you'd like to change:

Best thing you've done this year:

Worst thing you've done this year:

If you were a popular song you'd be called:

If you were the latest dance you'd be called:

There's a treasure in your attic.
      What is it?
      What will you do with it?

Will reader like or dislike this character? Why?

Any other reader response?

Your image of yourself
      At the beginning of the story:
      At the end of the story:

Look at the sample story, "The Clown." The writer took the idea from two things on the chart: She was a "tall, blond girl who wore a smile as if she had invented it," and "She always wanted to be a clown."

THE CLOWN

She was a tall, blond girl who wore a smile as if she had invented it. But somehow it was hard for people to believe the smile was real.

"I never trust anyone who smiles all the time," said a boy she'd just met. Right away she knew he could never be a part of her life.

"Not trust me!" She stomped her foot. How tacky, she thought. I'll show him. I'll show the world! She had always done the things she wanted to do. This was one reason she smiled a lot. She had always wanted to be a clown.

So in the next audition for the Ringling Brothers circus she hurried down to try out. She had been a closet clown for most of her life, so she was bursting with confidence.

She started to worry, though, when the other people who were trying out did back flips and cartwheels. They tossed each other in the air. They fell out of old cars and off trampolines and tightropes.

"What can you do?" asked the head clown, who was running the auditions.

She thought and thought. She thought of the boy who didn't like people to smile all the time. Maybe everyone was like him. Maybe people, those who were honest, liked people who looked unhappy. It made them feel better.

"I can look sad," she said, and proceeded to do so.

"Is that all?" he asked.

She was worried, but she said, "Yes." He didn't know how hard that was for a happy person to do.

"Can you look sad when everyone in the audience is laughing at you?" he asked.

"Yes," she said.

"Can you look sad when all the other clowns are laughing and trying to make you laugh?"

"Yes, I can," she said, and she showed him.

"You are a very sad clown," he admitted. "You must be very unhappy. You must have had a very sad life. You need to have some fun. You're hired."

She looked so sad at the news that he laughed and laughed. She felt like laughing, too, and she did. But only on the inside.

LOOKING OVER YOUR JOURNAL ENTRIES FOR STORIES

Read back over your journal. You have already looked at fantasies to write about. What else can you find?

Humor. You find a piece about a funny or very embarrassing moment. Write a situation comedy for television using this incident. You are the star, of course, but there are other characters on the show. Write the script. Pretend it's happening while you write.

Mystery. Think of something you have lost or misplaced. Write a mystery about hunting for and finding this object. Or write an adventure using the lost object as the main character. A friend went on a long trip. When she returned a huge blue bear that sat on her bed was gone. She could never discover what happened to Blue Bear. But she could write a story about finding it after following up clues. Or she could write about Blue Bear's adventures wherever he went and find out if he got lonely for her. Is there a place where lost toys go? What would this place be like? Is it the same place where lost socks go? What do the toys do with all those lost socks?

Magic. You wrote a piece that compared your life to a patchwork quilt. Think of the magic words for writers: What if?

What if there were something magic about that quilt? You could sew in a piece and what that piece represented would then happen. What problems could this cause? If you took out a piece, it would disappear from your life. What problems could this cause?

Your committee in stories. You have done the exercise where you identified all the people inside you. What if your committee were stranded on an island and had to survive? Write that story. Each committee member is a character. What problems could you have?

Your committee wins a trip aboard one of those luxurious ocean liners. As soon as you get on the trip, one of your committee disappears. What happened to him or her? Can you find this member? Write this mystery.

Your committee accidently gets lost in time. Did you go back in time or forward in time? What happens? How do you get back or adjust to living there?

Pet stories. Use pets you have had or have now as main characters in stories. Think of the traits they have and how those traits could get them in trouble. Think of all the different kinds of stories you could write: mystery, adventure, comedy, true-to-nature. Maybe you could imagine something like this: Your dog goes camping with you. While you're in the woods, he gets lost. Write the adventure of what happens to him and how he gets home.

Your cat has this bad habit of climbing up into the top of a tree and becoming frightened so you have to get her down. After several times you say, "Okay, stay there until you learn to climb down by yourself." Two days later she comes in looking funny. She never climbs in a tree again. What happened to her? Did she step off on a low-flying cloud and have a scary adventure? Did the tree or things that live in it frighten her or teach her something?

Your tomcat and the tomcat across the street fight all the time. One night both of them disappear. They don't come back for a week. When they return they both look tattered and exhausted and they are the best of friends. What happened to them?

More about stories. Almost any of your journal entries of past events could become a story. Expand and make up parts you don't remember about these events. Change parts you didn't like so that the story suits you better. Authors quite often draw on their own lives for their novels. They take pieces of their lives and write them over again. They make them better or much different. While it doesn't change what really happens, it gives the author a chance to experience things that could have happened.

FICTION AND YOUR FAMILY

You are fighting with your mother or father all the time. It seems as if all your family does is fight. Write a story in which your family goes on a vacation. You are backpacking in the mountains, sailing in the Caribbean, or exploring caves in Arkansas. Something goes wrong. A family member or the whole family becomes lost. Your boat sinks and you have to swim to an island and live until you are rescued. You could turn the story into fantasy by having your family step through a time warp and go forward or backward into time. Imagine your entire family having to survive when there are dinosaurs all around you. You could be sucked under the ocean into a hidden city. You could step into an alternate world while exploring underground.

Would you still fight while on this adventure? The real personality of each individual would come out. Who would be the strongest and help most? Who would continue to cause trouble? Would you all have to work together eventually to survive?

You and your sister or brother share a room at home. You fight all the time. You can't seem to share anything without a quarrel. On a trip into Mexico, someone kidnaps both of you. Write the story of how you escape and get back to your family.

One of your grandparents is put into a nursing home, but you feel that he or she doesn't belong there. Write a story telling how you kidnap and take the grandparent on one last adventure. Does another of the occupants in the nursing home come along? What if all of them want to escape and you are in charge of this escapade? Would you still be the leader? What problems would you have?

Describe a close encounter of the family kind. You and your family are driving to visit someone. You are stopped by a flying saucer landing in front of you on the road. The aliens take you into the saucer and interview you. What would they want to know? They take you to visit their planet. What would it be like? Would you be frightened? How about the rest of your family? Would you talk together before you told them anything? Would you hold a family conference to decide what was safe to eat and do, and to plan how to get back to your car?

FAMILY FICTION

Some rainy day or boring TV night, talk your family into writing stories together. Each person has a sheet of paper. Each person writes the beginning of a story. Each writing period is timed. When the timer buzzes, pass your story to the right. Take up the story where the person before you left off and continue it. When every person has contributed to every story, read them aloud. After you are finished, write in your journal about this experience. Was it fun? Who was the best storyteller? The worst? Who wrote the funniest parts? The saddest? Who was the most creative, had the most imagination?

SCIENCE FICTION

Look back when you wrote some time machine pieces in your journal. For instance, if you wrote that a chapter of your life was saving the president, fictionalize that adventure and write about it in detail. You may have already done this in part to tell about the happening, but now write an entire story with beginning, middle, and end. Use sensory images and good description. Put in other people so that you have dialogue. *Show* the story, don't *tell* it as you may have done earlier.

THE MILLIONAIRE

You have won a million dollars in a contest, but there is one catch. You can't spend this money on yourself. Write a story about spending it on someone close to you. Or write a story about spending it on total strangers who need it. Write out the details of how you'd do this, how the other people would react or feel, and how you'd feel.

TRAVEL STORIES

You win a travel agency contest. You can travel anyplace in the world free for a year. Each time you go someplace you can take one person with you. There has to be a good reason for taking this particular person on this particular trip. What trips would you make? Who would you take on each trip? Write some stories about these trips.

You might first make a list (see page 150) of the people you know and where you think they'd like or need to go.

Person	Place	Reason
Mother	Climbing trip to Kilimanjaro	She loves to hike. [Porters would carry everything and cook all the meals.]
Father	Super Bowl	He could be on the field and help coach. He coaches all the time from his chair in front of the TV.
My sister	Rome	One of the big dress designers would use her for a model and she'd get a new wardrobe. She loves clothes.
My brother	Jungles of Brazil	He's a survival fanatic in Scouts. He thinks having to survive some place would be fun. He could find out. It might not be so much fun. I wouldn't go with him when he got lost.

THE SILLIES

A magician comes along and turns each person you know into a bird. Write a poem about some of them, remembering that the bird has a name. Now the magician has changed them into animals. Do the same writing. Oh, no, now he's changed them into fish. Write some fish stories or poetry.

The Redheaded Teacher Bird

"Study, study," calls this bird.
Giving lessons so absurd.
Counting berries,
Adding bugs,
Dividing worms,
Multiplying slugs.
Reading weather,
Building nests,
Grooming feathers.
What strange tests.
I have to know where beetles hide,
When to flap and when to glide,
I have to build a nest that's strong,
Losing points when things go wrong.
I can't complain at recess, though,
We play at chasing magpie and crow.
It's not my usual fourth grade class.
Flying high's the way to pass.

It might be fun to share some of these poems if you don't give away too many secret feelings in writing them.

CONCLUSION

You could probably write a story or poem about everything that happens to you. Remember not to get mixed up about what is fact and what is fiction. Your teacher might not understand what you are talking about if you went in and said, "Thanks for teaching me how to divide worms yesterday." Your dad might look at you strangely if you said, "Did you enjoy your trip to the Super Bowl?" Your sister might not lend you her new Italian design sweater.

But writing fiction about your life can help you understand it better. It can help you escape when you need to. It will make your thinking more creative when you have to deal with real-life situations, solve real problems with people in your life, or stop being angry at someone for little reasons that are your fault. The more you write about people—fact or fiction—the more you will understand them.

Someday you might decide you'd like to write stories as a hobby, or maybe even write and sell them. You will certainly have a storehouse of ideas in your journal.

*A well-written Life is almost as rare as
a well-spent one.*
— Thomas Carlyle
Essays

*Fiction reveals truths that reality
obscures.*
— Jessamyn West

POINTS TO REMEMBER

- Most writers keep a journal.

- Your past journal entries are an excellent source for your fiction writing.

- You can discover truths when you are writing fiction.

- The journal is a place to practice writing fiction.

- The more you write about people, the better you will understand them.

- Writing fiction about your life can help you understand yourself better.

CHAPTER 13

Rereading Your Journal

*We read often with as much talent as
we write.*

—Ralph Waldo Emerson
Journals

INTRODUCTION

Rereading one's journal carefully, thoughtfully, and compassionately brings the act and art of journal keeping full circle. Rereading gives us a chance to go back — to relive past experiences and to recall forgotten events. Rereading also helps in the process of self-discovery. We find patterns in our experiences, plots in our life stories. Reviewing what has gone before can show us where we've been, where we are now, and, perhaps, an idea of where we might be going.

PURPOSES AND AIMS

- To review personal experiences in a nonjudgmental way

- To remember both glad and sad occasions and events

- To discover that we can learn from failure as well as from success

- To find patterns in our feelings, attitudes, and responses

- To set new personal goals

GETTING READY TO REREAD YOUR JOURNAL

Rereading your journal is a lot like reclimbing a mountain:

- It was hard, but I learned a lot about hiking that first time up.

- This path doesn't seem as steep or as rocky as it did before.

- The other time I was so busy finding my way I never noticed the trees, the lake, the other mountains.

- I can see now that I deserved some credit for making that first climb.

Just as there are ways to get the most out of a hike or a mountain climb, there are ways to get the most out of rereading your journal.

How to reread. First and most important, reread your journal with kindness and acceptance for the person you were when you wrote those earlier entries. Read with thoughtfulness but without harsh judgment.

As you begin, you may find that your rereading makes you feel uncomfortable:

- How could I have been so stupid!

- I don't want to read about when Baxter died.

- I was so excited over such an unimportant little thing.

- Me! Me! Me! You'd think no one else lived around here.

Remember, you wrote those entries when you were *there, then.* That is where you came from to reach *here* and *now.*

As you read, you may find that you expressed one belief or idea at one time and quite the opposite at another. You have every right to do so. A journal is not supposed to be the final word on a subject. It is a record of the way you feel, see, think at a certain time. In his long poem, *Song of Myself,* Walt Whitman wrote:

> *Do I contradict myself?*
> *Very well then I contradict myself,*
> *(I am large, I contain multitudes.)*

◻ ◻ ◻

In your reading be watching for ways that you have changed. Watch, too, for patterns in your feelings, attitudes, and observations. Your past can help you with your todays.

When to read. When to reread your journal will be up to you. You may, from time to time, turn through it, reading an entry here and there. Some people reread the entries of the previous day or two just before writing. But for serious study, most people choose a certain time for rereading—at the end of a month, after several months, or even once a year.

Reading the entries over a period of time longer than a week or two will give you a larger picture in which to see your daily life, to find patterns, and to discover yourself.

RELIVING EXPERIENCES

One of the joys of rereading your journal will be living over again happy occasions. You might even find some that, although you wrote about them, you had forgotten. You will also come across good experiences that both can and cannot be repeated. After you've found some of these happy experiences, choose one and write about your present feelings concerning it.

Last night I was reading an "I Remember ..." that I wrote last fall about going for picnics on Green Hill when I was a little kid. I got to thinking about how long it had been since I was out there. So, after school today I hiked out to the lane that goes up to the hill. We used to have such fun pretending that we were exploring that little dirt road. In summer there were wildflowers and tall grass and bushes—places to hide wild animals that might leap out and attack us. Well, up on Green Hill the wildflowers are blooming and the bushes are turning green. There's still a great view of the mountains and the river. But the little dirt road has been paved. There are houses on both sides. Where the flowers and bushes used to grow there are cement curbs. The hill is still the way it was but it won't last. They'll be building on it before long. So I'd better go up there again before it's changed. But whatever they do, they'll not be able to take away the memories I've written about.

You will, of course, find entries about unhappy, upsetting, or angry times, too. You may feel the need to write more about those times and those feelings, looking at them from where you are now.

DISCOVERING YOURSELF

Rereading your journal will reward you with insights about yourself. These insights are extremely valuable for your self growth.

What you remember and what your journal tells you. As you read back in your journal, you may be surprised to find that some of the things you have remembered are recorded quite differently. It can be that time and memory have played little tricks on you. Or it is also possible, especially where feelings are involved, that you wrote the way you did for a reason. Such an entry might be a subject for developing.

Me Now: I've been reading your entries for those two weeks on Uncle Pete's farm. You know, I was there too and what you wrote certainly isn't the way I saw things.

Me Then: Maybe you don't remember it right.

Me Now: No, I remember how I felt and that's not what you wrote.

Me Then: You know perfectly well Mom thought a visit to the farm would be something wonderful for me.

Me Now: I know all that. I know she couldn't really afford the plane fare, either, but even if you didn't — *especially* if you didn't — let her know how awful the two weeks were, you could have told your journal how you felt.

Me Then: Well....

Me Now: Were you afraid somebody would read it?

Me Then: Maybe. Sort of. No, not really. It's kind of hard to explain.

Me Now: Try me.

Me Then:	I guess I thought if I wrote that Uncle Pete and Aunt Whoosis were nice and their kids — *her* kids — were little angels and that I loved being nursemaid and cleaning lady and thought the smell of barns and pigpens was wonderful and so on *and so on* AND SO ON, I'd make myself begin to believe it.
Me Now:	Boy were you ever stu — —
Me Then:	Hey, I thought we weren't going to call names and say mean things.
Me Now:	Sorry, I forgot. It's just — you're supposed to be *honest* in your journal.
Me Then:	Well — I didn't really *plan* to be dishonest about it — it was, well, I was trying to — I guess you'd say I was trying to be loyal to Mom and I couldn't do that and be loyal to me and my journal too — or something.
Me Now:	Yeah, I see what you're saying and I'm going to have to do some more thinking about it.

Looking at the mistakes. Although you promise yourself to review your journal in an accepting way, still it is easy to become impatient with what you read. Remember that we aren't born knowing everything. We all have to learn as we go.

Ivan Southall, in his book *A Journey of Discovery*,* points out that not only must we be scared to be brave, but we must also know weakness to know strength, and we must be foolish to be wise.

> *We learn wisdom from failure much more than from success. We often discover what* will *do, by finding out what will not do; and probably he who never made a mistake never made a discovery.*
>
> — Samuel Smiles
> *Self-Help*

◻ ◻ ◻

When you find an entry that makes you feel annoyed or impatient with yourself, ask, What have I learned? What have I discovered?

Yesterday I wrote _____

Today I see _____

---

*Southall, Ivan. *A Journey of Discovery: On Writing for Children.* New York: Macmillan, 1975. P. 93.

> From where I stand now that seems like a dumb thing to have done—but from where I was standing then it seemed like the only thing to do. I guess the point is—now, six months later, I am standing in a different place. I *think* that means I'm moving along, making progress maybe? I'll look back again six months from now.

Change. One of the first things you'll notice as you reread are the changes—changes in how you write, what you write, even changes in your handwriting. (Does your handwriting vary according to the mood you're in?)

> When I started this journal I only made lists. Lists of what I did each day, lists of people, lists of how I felt. Gradually those lists grew into sentences, then into little paragraphs, and now I write whole pages. Even my handwriting is easier, smoother. It took me a long time to get acquainted and comfortable with my journal.

> At first I wasn't honest in my journal writing. It wasn't that I was trying to make up a different kind of life. It was because I thought somebody might read what I wrote and if I put down how I really felt and what I was thinking I'd get laughed at.

> My first journal writing was like writing assignments to hand in. I was writing for the teacher and for the class. I tried to say things the way she'd want me to or—awful—to impress them. I still have to remind myself that I'm writing for me and just me. I think I'm doing better.

Watch for other changes in your writing. Do your early entries read like a ship's log, recording only the facts? Have you learned to include observations about people and about the world around you? Are you using more sensory writing, describing how things look, sound, smell, taste, and feel? Are you learning to write about your feelings? Do you go beyond just recording the events of your day to examining them as well? Are you looking for the *how* and *why* and *what* to add to the *who* and *when* and *where* of your entries?

Are you doing any experimental writing in your journal—trying fantasy, turning entries into poems, making stories out of journal ideas?

As you watch for the changes in your writing, you will begin to notice other details about how, why, and what you write. You will find that your life is more than just a hodge-podge of unrelated events.

PATTERNS

Do you write in your journal every day, on certain days of the week, or just now and then? Do you see a pattern in the times you write and the times you don't write? Are you using your journal only when you are upset, angry, unhappy? Or are those the times you don't want to write? Can you find a pattern in when you use your journal?

Another pattern to look for lies in the things you write about and the things you don't write about. Is your journal like the sundial mentioned earlier, counting only the sunny hours?

Do you write only about yourself, or do you also write about other people?

Do you write only about your activities, where you go, things you do, or do you also write about what you are thinking and wondering?

Do you include wishes, hopes, plans, dreams in your entries, or do you write only about what has already happened?

There is nothing wrong with writing about yourself and what you do, or writing only about what you think or feel or hope or dream. But you will learn more about yourself if you write about the different sides and aspects of yourself and if you try writing about new topics and ideas now and then.

After you've noted the things you write about, read carefully to see *how* you write about them. Do your entries show that you usually write when you are excited or happy about something? Or do they reflect your anger, hurt feelings, or depression? Do you seem to be looking at the world in a positive or negative way?

> One day Mr. Ryan held up a sheet of paper. It was a big square and it had a little bitty hole in the middle of it. "Write down what you see," he told us. Then he asked, "How many of you wrote down *a big piece of paper with a little hole in it*?" Five kids raised their hands. Then he asked, "How many of you wrote *a little hole in the middle of a big piece of paper*?" The other fifteen of us raised our hands. Mr. Ryan told us, "That little hole isn't anywhere near the size of the square of paper, but that's what most of you saw first. You're probably the same ones who look up and see one little gray storm cloud instead of all the rest of the bright blue sky." In rereading my journal I am discovering that a lot of the time I only see the little storm cloud instead of the big blue sky.

> Today I heard something that has started me thinking. (Wow!) A woman on a talk show said, You see what you look for. You don't see what you don't look for. At first I thought Jeez, what a dumb thing to say. Then when I was reading over some of the things I wrote in my journal last winter I decided that I was looking for the down side of things a lot of the time and never once looked for the good things that were happening.

What do the patterns of your writing tell you about what you see and what you are looking for? Do you habitually look at the gloomy side or at the bright side? Or do you include both in your writing?

What other patterns are you finding? Are you quick to make judgments, does it take you a long time to make up your mind, or do you often let others make up your mind for you?

> In reading over my impressions of the new people I've met this year, I think maybe I'm too quick in making up my mind. Several times I've found that people I thought were wonderful at first weren't very nice when I got to know them, and then people I didn't think I liked at all have become my friends.

Do you seem to be a person who *makes* things happen or who *lets* things happen? If you are inclined to just let things happen to you, would you like to take charge now and then?

> I didn't realize how much I have been letting Nan influence the way I feel about myself and other people and *things* until I started rereading my journal. I've discovered that she is always—well, too often anyway—telling *me* what *I think*. She says You know you don't want to go with those kids. You won't have any fun with them. And she says You're not really mad at me, you just don't understand how other people feel. When she started taking psychology, first she told me Your problem is you don't think you deserve to be liked. And then the very next week (they must have started a new chapter in the psychology book) she told me Your problem is you think you're too special to have ordinary people for your friends. And from what I wrote in my journal I can see that *I believed what she was telling me*! I'm going to watch out for people telling me how to think and what to think. Journal keeping has helped me have a pretty good idea of *what I think* and I don't need other people trying to do it for me.

In chapter 3, "The Journal Records Today," you met members of the committee:

Dreamer	Cold-Water-Dasher
Leader	Stubborn Self
Artist	Nice Self
Scaredy-Cat	Optimist

Do these people show up in your journal? Do you give each of them a chance to be heard now and then? Are one or two of them taking over and never letting the others have a turn at expressing how they feel? Sometimes the Dreamer or Stubborn Self, or even the Nice Self, might need a little cold water dashed on them. The Leader should give the Scaredy-Cat a turn, and once in awhile the Dreamer and the Artist could put Cold-Water-Dasher in his place. From time to time try giving all sides of yourself a chance to express feelings and thoughts.

As you discover and think about patterns in your journal writing, are you finding that you want to encourage some of them and discourage others? Journal rereading time can also be a good time for setting new personal goals.

GOALS

Problems. In rereading your journal you have had a chance to see how you solved problems and met challenges in the past. Sometimes your methods worked, sometimes—you see now—you could have done better.

When I took the illustrations I made for *Animal Farm* in to show Miss T. she raved all over them and said they were wonderful. Then I asked her if once in awhile we could do our book reports in a different way, like my pictures. She looked at me real funny and said, I should have known you had *an ulterior motive in these.* Then she went on and said she'd been noticing how well I expressed myself in my drawings (did she mean the stuff I drew on my desk?), but she also felt that if I was willing to work on it I had the ability to express myself just as well with words. Outcome: She showed my pictures to the class and said if we checked it out with her she'd let us try other ways of doing book reports. And I told her I'd try a little harder on the writing.

I finally decided I needed some extra help with my math so I went in to see Ms. Jensen after school. She said I didn't need help, I was just lazy. I banged my math book on the floor and walked out.

As you read your entries, ask yourself:

- What would I do in that or a similar situation *now*?

- How can looking back at the way I handled problems before help me with other problems now?

- Do my problems seem to follow a pattern?

Since I threw my math book on the floor in Ms. Jensen's room I've been doing some thinking. Back when I was delivering papers I was mad at everybody one morning and threw a paper so hard it broke a window. And when Kevin kept on at me about missing all those free throws in the play-off game I got mad and threw his jeans in the shower. Maybe I should go out for baseball and get some credit for my throwing arm. I'm sure not doing myself any good with the way I'm throwing things now.

If you see unsatisfactory patterns in the way you handle problems, get along with people, or use your time, do you want to try to change those patterns? If you do, decide exactly what it is you want to change and state it in a positive way:

not   I don't want to throw things every time I get mad,

but   I want to learn to work off my anger in a helpful way.

not   I just won't have anything more to do with Nan,

but   I'm going to make myself speak up to Nan—in a nice but I-mean-it way—and tell her thanks but I can make some of my decisions for myself.

Steps in reaching a goal. These steps can help you reach your goals.

1. Look on the goal you set as an exciting challenge.

2. Watch out for those old *I-Can-t-Do-It* tapes. Look over some of your successes and make new tapes about those. (I did it that time, I can do it again.)

3. Rehearse your plans ahead of time. Write them out or write dialogues and imaginary encounters. Practice saying what you want to say until it comes easily. (Thank you, Nan, but ...) (If there won't always be a punching bag nearby, practice counting from one hundred to one for angry moments.)

4. Expect the best but, again, don't plan to climb the mountain in one leap. List small steps for reaching your goal.

5. Be your own person. Make your own decisions about your goal and take the responsibilities yourself.

Time.

> *To choose time is to save time.*
> —Francis Bacon
> *Essays*

> *An inch of time cannot be bought
> by an inch of gold.*
> —Chinese proverb

♩   ♩   ♩

Are you finding that your days aren't long enough to do all the things you want to do, you have to do? Exactly what do you do with your time every day? One way to find out is to make an activity log in which you chart how you spend each hour of the day. If that seems too overwhelming, start by charting what you do from the end of your school day until bedtime.

After a week or so of logging in your activities and the actual time they take, look at your chart. Are you spending your time the way you really want to? Spending time doesn't necessarily mean filling up your day with busyness. Everyone needs some quiet time in which to relax and think.

When you have several charts that quite accurately show what you are doing each day, try evaluating *how* you are spending your time.

How much time do you spend alone? _____

How much time do you spend with other people? _____

Which activities do you do every day? _____

Which activities do you do often? _____

Which activities do you do seldom? _____

Which activities cost money? _____

Which activities don't cost money? _____

Which activities do you not like to do? _____

Which activities are you indifferent about? _____

Which activities would you like to do more often? _____

Does your activity log suggest goals to set concerning the way you spend your time or the way you would like to spend your time?

> *There is a time for some things, and a time for all things; a time for great things, and a time for small things.*
>
> —Miguel de Cervantes
> *Don Quixote*

◻ ◻ ◻

After reading. Rereading your journal may inspire you to set new personal goals, to use your time differently, and to give careful thought to your relationships with the people around you. But you aren't rereading just to find things about yourself and your life that you want to improve. There are pleasures to find in rereading, too.

We have already talked about reliving experiences. Another pleasure is to find entries in your journal that beg to be used for stories, poems, songs. There are passages within your journal that will make you pause and say, Did I really write that? I never dreamed I could put those feelings into words and do it so perfectly. Yes, you'll find little gems of writing as you reread, gems that you may or may not wish to share.

After rereading, you might want to make notes about some of the patterns you have discovered, patterns of yourself or of your writing. Some journal keepers write summaries, overviews, or observations about their feelings and reactions to what they have read.

As I come to more recent entries, I find I can't be as objective. But in realizing that, accepting that I'm still too close to this month's happenings, I also realize that with time I have learned to look on other emotional happenings as part of learning: how to do things, get along with people, accept myself. I think there are some old sayings like *Time heals* and *Time teaches*. Next year at this time I may be able to look at what happened to me last week and say

I LEARNED A LOT

I BEGAN TO GROW UP A LITTLE THEN

Maybe — but I'm not promising.

CONCLUSION

Rereading one's journal can be painful, amusing, entertaining, rewarding. Looking back should be as much for seeing what we've been thinking, how we've changed or not changed, how we've grown, and what we've done right as for finding what we can do better. Always, rereading is a chance to reacquaint ourselves with the thoughts we remember putting down and to rediscover the ones we've forgotten. Overall, rereading shows us how we've come along our personal paths, and it gives us some guidance as to how we should continue.

POINTS TO REMEMBER

- *It makes me laugh to read over this diary.
  It's so full of contradictions....*
  —Sophie Tolstoy

- Keep in mind as you reread a passage, *that* is where you were then in order to be where you are now. Be kind to yourself.

- It is your prerogative to change your mind now and then. It is your prerogative *not* to change your mind—now and then.

- Look for patterns in what you write about and in when, why, and how you write.

- You sometimes learn from your victories as well as from your defeats and mistakes.

- Rereading your journal helps you look for challenges—to make changes, to set new goals, and to learn even more about the main character, *you*.

SUGGESTED READING

Capacchione, Lucia. *The Creative Journal: The Art of Finding Yourself.* Athens, Ohio: Swallow Press, Ohio University Press, 1979. See especially "Reviewing Your Journal."

Jackson, Jacqueline. *Turn Not Pale, Beloved Snail.* Boston: Little, Brown, 1974. Chapter 10, "My Best Thoughts."

Rainer, Tristine. *The New Diary.* Los Angeles: Jeremy P. Tarcher, 1978. Chapter 13, "Rereading the Plot of Your Life."

CHAPTER 14

Sharing the Journal

*Words that may become alive and walk up and
down in the hearts of the hearers....*

—Rudyard Kipling
(Speech, Royal Academy Banquet,
London, 1906)

INTRODUCTION

Rereading one's journal is an important and necessary step in getting the greatest good out of journal keeping. Sharing from one's journal is not necessary, but it can be the source of one of the greatest pleasures of journal keeping.

Journal sharing can be reading one sentence to one person, reading a paragraph to a small group, or rewriting a passage for many to read. The first step will probably be student-teacher sharing as mentioned in chapter 2, "Techniques and Definitions." The sharing of an entry or two might possibly lead to a student-teacher dialogue journal in which ideas and observations, questions and comments are passed back and forth. As willingness to share begins to grow, everyone involved must always keep in mind that reading or listening to another's journal thoughts has to be done in an accepting, non-judgmental way. As emphasized in chapter 2, *sharing someone's journal is a privilege; a confidence cannot be shouted to the crowd.*

PURPOSES AND AIMS

- To discover the worth of one's own writing

- To learn to feel comfortable sharing certain personal ideas or thoughts

- To discover journal material suitable for rewriting, enlarging, or developing into essays, poems, or stories

- To discover journal material for rewriting into gifts for others

BEGINNING TO SHARE

The poet W. H. Auden said that he liked hanging around words, listening to what they say. The pleasure of writing, of listening to what words have to say, doesn't depend on sharing with an audience. However, sometimes you will write a sentence, develop an idea, or record something you have felt, seen, or heard with such style or aptly created metaphor that you will want to share.

When you write in your journal you are not writing for an audience but only for yourself. However, as you reread your journal, you may find many things that would interest or help others.

Today I was rereading what I wrote a year ago—just before starting junior high. I am going to copy for Stacy what I wrote the day before school started and then some of the things I wrote during that first week and month. Then she can see that she's not the only person scared to death at the thought of junior high and she'll also see that most of the things I was scared of or worried about never happened—or if they did, they weren't big deals.

Sharing may be reading just one line to someone who already shares your sense of humor, your love of L. M. Boston books, your bird-watching or bottle-collecting passion. But it can also be more than reading aloud what you've already written.

As you read an entry you like to others or reread it to yourself, think about different ways you might be able to use that same passage. Could you develop it into a somewhat longer personal essay? By asking What if? could you turn it into the plot for a story? With some rearrangement of words could it become a poem?

POETRY

Poetry can be a subject filled with technical terms like *metre* and *scansion, hexameter, dipody,* and *iambic, dactylic,* or *trochaic.* Poetry can also be simple words, written with personal feeling, to help ourselves (and others) see things as we've never quite seen them before.

In chapter 8, you tried clustering with the words *change, risk,* and *possibilities.* Use some of the terms from your clustering to make a poem. Here's an example using *possibilities*:

> Possibilities — hopes, plans, maybe, realization,
> expectations, perhaps, questions

> > Possibilities are
> > questions,
> > are bright-faced plans.

> > Possibilities are
> > maybe — someday — perhaps.

> > Possibilities are expectations
> > that become realizations.

Experiment with turning a sentence or two into a poem form. Decide which words you'll use and which words won't be necessary. Think about where you'll divide the lines to give emphasis and rhythm to what you are saying.

> > This morning the sun shone through the
> > prisms in the kitchen window and it turned
> > Angel into a rainbow cat.

> > > This morning
> > > the sun shone through
> > > the window prisms
> > > turning
> > > Angel
> > > into a rainbow cat.

Practice in changing prose into poetry can help all of your writing in at least two ways. It will make you more aware of writing that flows smoothly and is easy to read, and it will help you to notice ways of using descriptive, colorful, picture-making words.

A college professor, William M. White, has taken material from Henry David Thoreau's journals and arranged it into books of nature poems. (See Suggested Reading, Thoreau and White.) Professor White did not change or leave out a single word or punctuation mark that Thoreau had used, but by rearranging the prose lines of some of Thoreau's journal passages, he has been able to make us see the poetry in the naturalist's writings. Of course, Professor White was working with the material of a man who, over almost a quarter of a century, had written two million words of journal entries. The professor's versions of those journal entries prove that sometimes prose is poetry.

Paul Fleischman, author of the Newbery Award-winning *Joyful Noise: Poems for Two Voices*, writes prose that is poetic — flowing and musical and rich with imagery and metaphor. He also tells first-class stories. See Suggested Reading for other books by Paul Fleischman.

Subjects for poetry. Sometimes we are inclined to think that poetry can be only about serious subjects like life, death, friendship, or love, or about beautiful or artistic things. But poems are written about any subject. Rhoda Bacmeister wrote a poem about galoshes (Arbuthnot and Root, *Time for Poetry*, page 3), and Eve Merriam has written about windshield wipers (Merriam, *Out Loud*, page 3). Beatrice Janosco wrote a poem called "The Garden Hose," in which she pictures the hose as if it were a snake in her garden (Dunning et al., *Reflectings on a Gift of Watermelon Pickles*, page 110).

You don't have to limit your poetry to descriptions of people, places, animals, or things. You can turn happenings, big or small, into poetry, too.

Myrle and I went out to the county fair today. We wandered around looking at flowers and quilts and a life-sized cow carved out of butter. Myrle wanted to see the livestock and I don't mind the sheep and pigs but going into those barns with the horses and cows — well, they're all so BIG and I'm afraid of their hooves. Then we went outside to see the pheasants and ducks and things. They were in great high pens made of flimsy chicken wire. There was a sort of narrow alley between the rows of pens and a cowboy came riding through there leading a steer on a long, long rope. The steer went charging back and forth and there was no place for us to go. We pushed ourselves up against the wire cages but the steer bumped us and then it went on. I head a woman say, Look at that girl, she's as white as a sheet. We came home pretty soon after that.

Once my best friend and I went to the County Fair.
We walked into a narrow alley
between chicken-wire-fenced pens
that held fancy pheasants
    short-toed ducks
    and you name it.
As we looked at pheasants' feathers and ducks' toes
a cowboy came riding through leading a steer on a rope.
The rope was so long,
the alley so narrow,
the steer so wild,
that it rushed right at us.
The fence was too flimsy to climb
    too high to jump over
    too big to run around.
As I closed my eyes
I felt the steer's breath on my neck,
his body brushing my back.
That experience taught me something.
    Don't get caught in narrow alleys?
    Beware of steers on long ropes?
    Never trust a cowboy?
No.
It taught me that when
you close your eyes
for the last time —
sometimes you get the chance to open them again.

To rhyme or not to rhyme. As you know, poetry doesn't have to rhyme, but sometimes it can be fun to work out rhyming verse. Experimenting with rhyming words is like figuring out a puzzle. Remember, though, rhymes and rhythm must never become more important than the thought and idea of the poem.

Tonight just before I went to bed I saw the possum in the mulberry tree again. Somehow he missed a branch and fell out of the tree, all the way down into Mother's flower bed. I don't know if possums can be embarrassed but this poor little guy sure acted as if he was.

    I saw you, possum,
    in the mulberry tree.
    I saw you climb
    and I saw you fall
    and I saw you slink away
    as if
        your mother
           had said
             Shame!

> Our little possum is hanging his head.
> From a high-up branch he leaned to see,
> He lost his balance, he missed the tree,
> He lit with a thump in the lily bed.
> Our little possum is hanging his head.

For more on how to write poetry see chapter 10 of *Creative Writing: A Handbook for Teaching Young People* (Phillips and Steiner).

For ideas of how poets write and what they write about, look at the poetry collections listed in the Suggested Reading section at the end of this chapter.

PROSE

As suggested earlier, you can discover in your journal ideas and material for essays, short stories, and even reports. Your ideas and feelings about the future or past of your school, neighborhood, town, and country—plans, activities, and controversies—can be of interest to your classmates, who will have their own ideas on those subjects.

The thoughts you have recorded in your journal might be the beginning of a longer piece of writing on one of those topics. Your opinion could be written to be read to others, to appear as an essay in your school magazine, or to be an editorial in the school newspaper. A short piece might be a letter to the editor for a newspaper or magazine.

Chapter 12, "Using Your Journal to Practice Fiction," has already shown you ways to develop stories from your journal ideas. You can read your stories aloud, submit them to class or school newspapers or magazines, or, if your school has a publishing center, you can have your story made into a permanently bound book.

What about the odds and ends of interesting information you've collected in your journal? Magazines and newspapers publish feature articles and human interest stories. Did you do any census taking as suggested in chapter 11, "The All-About-People Journal"? If so, consider the following activities:

- Write a *Did You Know?* article or make a list of interesting facts you discovered about your school or town.

- Pick out short, interesting bits of information, letter them on separate cards or pieces of colored paper, and use them for bulletin board displays: A FACT A DAY; FOR YOUR INFORMATION; DID YOU KNOW?; BET YOU NEVER GUESSED.

- Write a feature article about some other interesting things you learned as you were asking your census-taking questions.

    When I asked the neighbors on my block how many loaves of bread they ate in a year, four people said How on earth would I know?, one said Are you working for the bakery?, and one said Good heavens, it's bad enough I eat all that bread—I don't want everyone to know how much!

A FAMILY ALBUM

In chapter 4, "The Journal Remembers the Past," you tried different ways of remembering people and events in your own past. Now collect some of those memories for a family book. Ask other members of your family to share their memories and stories, too.

Some chapter headings for The Family Album could include:

- Earliest Memories
- Places We've Lived
- Pets
- Vacations
- Holidays
- Family Customs and Traditions
- Favorite Books
- Favorite Music
- Ancestors
- Family Stories

GIFTS

> The only gift is a portion of thyself ...
> therefore the poet brings his poem ...
> the painter, his picture....
> —Ralph Waldo Emerson
> *Essays: Gifts*

Family books. One of the most thoughtful and gratifying ways of sharing your journal is to give portions of it as a gift.

Instead of making The Family Album mentioned in the preceding section a cooperative project, you might do it alone or with the help of brothers or sisters as a gift for parents or grandparents. Or you might prefer to put together a book devoted to just one subject. Any of the chapter headings suggested for The Family Album could be a book in itself:

- The Phillips Family Christmas Book
- Our Birthday Book
- A Book about Baxter
- Do You Remember?

For your eyes only. Another idea would be to assemble a selection of your own thoughts and memories, plus incidents, plans, and dreams shared with another person, and present it as a gift to that special person. That person could be your best friend, one or both parents, your grandparents, a younger brother or sister, an older brother or sister about to leave home, or a special teacher.

You can find beautifully bound blank books in book, stationery, gift, and greeting card stores. Or you might prefer to make your own book to copy your journal excerpts into.

Another way to share the selections you've chosen would be to make a picture, quilt, or collage of them.

For Marcy

This word picture is made from entries in my journal:
The mountains are those plots and plans we've dreamed together:

"Marcy and I are going to be actresses when we grow up ..."; "Marcy and I are going to earn enough money this summer to buy a whole bunch of new clothes ..."; "Marcy and I...."

Those dark clouds are the dark times we've had:

"I'll never speak to Marcy again ..."; "Marcy hates me, I know she does...."

And that flowered meadow is the fun we've had together....

Other gifts. Look through your journal for brief observations, interesting facts, metaphors you especially like, or passages to turn into poems. Find comments you have made about particular subjects such as music, books, trips, or hobbies. Use these collections to personalize calendars, blank books, or record books as gifts for special people.

For example, if you are a bird watcher, a weather watcher, an explorer and hiker, your journal may have entries that could make a highly personal nature book or calendar. Following are some observations of the type that could be used. These are from the journals of Henry David Thoreau.

About Birds

[Eagles] *While one is circling this way, another circles that. Kites without strings.*
September 16, 1852

I hear the bluebirds.... Their short warble trilled in the air reminding of so many corkscrews.
March 18, 1853

This is the gospel according to the wood thrush.
He makes a Sabbath out of a week-day.
April 27, 1854

I hear now ... the note of the first red-wings,
like the squeaking of a sign.
April 2, 1856

One such description could be carefully written or lettered on the first page for each month or week of a record book, or all could be scattered randomly through the book, to come upon as a surprise. If you like to draw, you could add pen and ink sketches to illustrate some of your entries.

You might want to use longer passages, poems, or descriptive paragraphs such as the following, also from Thoreau's journals.

JANUARY

Every leaf and twig was this morning covered with a sparkling ice armor; even the grasses in exposed fields were hung with innumerable diamond pendants, which jingled merrily when brushed by the foot of the traveller.

FEBRUARY

It is whispered through all the aisles of the forest that another spring is approaching. The wood mouse listens at the mouth of his burrow, and the chickadee passes the news along.

MARCH

His Most Serene Birdship! His soft warble melts in the ear, as the snow is melting in the valleys around. The bluebird comes and with his warble drills the ice and sets free the rivers and ponds and frozen ground.

Your own personal greeting cards are another way to share writings from your journal. Use blank cards or illustrated cards that have no message. Choose passages that are appropriate for the occasion or season, or ones that you would like to share with the person you are sending the card to.

CONCLUSION

Don't feel that the thoughts you share with others must be profound philosophical statements or earthshaking discoveries. It will be your insight, your observances and reflections, your way of seeing ordinary day-to-day living that your friends will value.

> *I omit the unusual—the hurricanes and earthquakes— and describe the common. This has the greatest charm and is the true theme of poetry.*
>
> —Henry David Thoreau
> *Journal*, August 28, 1851

Recording, examining, experimenting, writing every day or once a week, filling a few lines or pages and pages—however you use your journal, the more you write and the better acquainted you and your journal become, the surer you will be that you have found a true and understanding friend.

> *What is a friend? I will tell you. It is one with whom you dare to be yourself.*
>
> —Paraphrased from Frank Crane
> "A Definition of Friendship"

POINTS TO REMEMBER

- Many incidents, observations, and descriptions in your journal can be developed into stories, personal essays, or poems.

- Many incidents involving family and friends will bring them pleasure when shared in a creative way.

- We are funnier, sillier, and more foolish than we might like to think.

  —Ralph Waldo Emerson
  "We Are Wiser Than We Know"
  Essays: The Over-Soul

- Be willing to share your wise ideas on occasion, but also share the funny and foolish ones.

- Journal keeping is a voyage of discovery. We make the trip alone, but we find things of value along the way to bring back, to treasure, and to share.

SUGGESTED READING

Arbuthnot, May Hill, and Shelton L. Root, Jr., eds. *Time for Poetry*, 3d ed. Glenview, Ill.: Scott, Foresman, 1968.

Dunning, Stephen, Edward Lueders, and Hugh Smith, eds. *Reflections on a Gift of Watermelon Pickles*. New York: Lothrop, Lee & Shepard, 1967.

_____. *Some Haystacks Don't Even Have Any Needle*. Glenview, Ill.: Scott, Foresman, 1969.

Fleischman, Paul. *Graven Images*. New York: Harper & Row, 1982.

_____. *The Half-a-Moon Inn*. New York: Harper & Row, 1980.

_____. *Joyful Noise: Poems for Two Voices*. New York: Harper & Row, 1988.

Hoffman, William J. *Life Writing: A Guide to Family Journals and Personal Memoirs*. New York: St. Martin's Press, 1982.

Knott, Leonard L. *Writing for the Joy of It*. Cincinnati: Writers Digest Books, 1983.

Merriam, Eve. *Out Loud*. New York: Atheneum, 1973.

_____. *A Word or Two with You*. New York: Atheneum, 1981.

O'Neill, Mary. *Hailstones and Halibut Bones*. New York: Doubleday, 1989.

_____. *Words Words Words*. Garden City, N.Y.: Doubleday, 1966.

Phillips, Kathleen, and Barbara Steiner. *Catching Ideas*. Englewood, Colo.: Libraries Unlimited, 1988.

_____. *Creative Writing: A Handbook for Teaching Young People*. Littleton, Colo.: Libraries Unlimited, 1985.

Stillman, Peter R. *Families Writing*. Cincinnati: Writer's Digest Books, 1989.

Thoreau, Henry David, and William M. White. *Sweet, Wild World*. Boston: Charles River Books, 1982.

Whiteley, Opal. Adapted by Jane Boulton. *Opal: The Journal of an Understanding Heart*. Palo Alto, Calif.: Tioga, 1984.

Index

About the Authors

BARBARA STEINER has published more than forty books for children, young adults, and teachers. For Libraries Unlimited she has coauthored two books with Kathleen Phillips: *Creative Writing: A Handbook for Teaching Young People* and *Catching Ideas*. Barbara has a Master's degree in Elementary Education with a major in Curriculum. She has taught third grade and was a reading specialist. She now teaches creative writing classes in Continuing Education at The University of Colorado, both Boulder and Denver campuses. She teaches workshops for children and teachers in the Rocky Mountain area and visits with children in the schools, talking about writing books.

She is a member of Colorado Author's League and was a charter member of the Rocky Mountain Chapter of Society of Children's Book Writers. After holding many offices in the local chapter as well as being regional advisor, she now serves on the National Board.

Both of the books for Libraries Unlimited have won the Top Hand Award from Colorado Author's League for best nonfiction textbook of the year.

KATHLEEN C. PHILLIPS, with a background of teaching, advertising, and library work, has published articles, stories, and poetry for both adults and children, two children's books, and, with coauthor Barbara Steiner, two adult mysteries (Zebra Books) in addition to Libraries Unlimited books, *Creative Writing: A Handbook for Teaching Young People* and *Catching Ideas*. Kathleen has taken part in Writers in the Schools workshops for the past dozen years and has taught adult workshops in Colorado, Nebraska, New Mexico, and Texas. She is a member of Denver Woman's Press Club, Colorado Author's League, has won the Author's League Top Hand Award for both articles and stories and, with Barbara Steiner, for *Creative Writing* and *Catching Ideas*. She is also an active member and Regional Advisor of the Rocky Mountain Chapter of the Society of Children's Book Writers.